Secrets of the Mouse

Alan Joyce

Table of Contents

About this Guide

Behind the Scenes at Disneyland

A visit to the "Happiest Place on Earth" is designed to be a magical experience for the young and the young at heart, but the most extraordinary part of the magic is the endless hard work and ingenuity that goes into creating it in the first place. From the smallest illusion to the grandest pyrotechnic effect, the magic of Disneyland is immeasurably more incredible when experienced from behind the scenes.

Every attraction in Disneyland is meticulously crafted by Disney Imagineers and completed by the performances and contributions of Cast Members. All the little touches that define the details of each attraction contribute to the guest experience as a whole and make the Disneyland experience all the more magical.

This guide is intended to be a look at the magic behind the magic, and will hopefully give the reader a greater appreciation for the incredible efforts and innovations that create the Disneyland experience. If seeing how a magic trick works spoils the fun for you, then you might want to try another guide. However, if you find yourself asking "How do they do that?" when you see an oncoming boulder in Indiana Jones or translucent ghosts in the Haunted Mansion, this guide is here to satisfy your curiosity.

About this Guide

Reading this Guide

This book is intended to be read non-linearly, and you will likely find it most convenient to look up an attraction in this guide while you are standing in line for it. Both the attraction pages and the Hidden Mickey lists are designed so that they can be referenced quickly and easily when appropriate, and the Queue Games section is included to keep you entertained during long waits in line.

As you make your plans, wander the pathways of Disneyland Park, or reminisce about Disneyland at home, I hope this guide will serve to both entertain you and enrich your Disneyland experience.

Contacting the Author

Any feedback is greatly appreciated, so feel free to send your questions or comments to the author via email at the address alan@secretsofthemouse.com.

How this Guide is Organized

Attractions

The Attractions section of this guide contains details of all the rides and shows that make up Disneyland Park. The attractions are organized first by the land in which they are located and then by alphabetical order. Each attraction has a summary, a look behind the scenes of the attraction, and a Things to Look For section. The Things to Look For section lists all of the little details and secrets that Disney Imagineers and Cast Members have added to attractions, but that are overlooked by most guests. It is also the place where you will find helpful hints and tips about the attractions. Photos or other visuals are also included for each attraction.

Hidden Mickeys

Sprinkled throughout all areas of the park are Hidden Mickeys, small tributes to the famous mouse who serves as the base of all Disney media. Usually consisting of the classic tri-circle Mickey symbol, Disney Imagineers and Cast Members incorporate Hidden Mickeys into everything from lanterns to roller coasters. Hunting for Hidden Mickeys can add a whole new dimension to a Disneyland visit, and it is always a surprise to discover these secret gems of Disneyland.

How this Guide is Organized

The Hidden Mickeys section of this guide lists some of the most notable Hidden Mickeys, organized like the attraction pages; first by the land in which they are located, and then by their more exact locations listed in alphabetical order. Each Hidden Mickey is accompanied by a picture or diagram, a description of its characteristics, and a score out of ten for its difficulty to find as well as its impressiveness.

Queue Games

Let's face it, no matter how much magic is in the air at Disneyland, there will always be attraction queues. A significant portion of the average Disneyland day is spent waiting in line, so why not transform the line experience into an opportunity to both have fun and learn more about your favorite attractions?

The Queue Games section contains scavenger hunts, puzzles, and other activities with varying levels of difficulty that directly relate to specific attractions. These activities are meant to be completed while waiting in the queue for the attraction, and you will often be able to find the necessary clues as you progress through the line. With the exception of the Roger Rabbit's Car Toon Spin game, all Queue Games can be done in either the FastPass or standby line. Queue Games are organized first by land and then by attraction listed in alphabetical order.

Attractions

Adventureland

Attractions

- Indiana Jones Adventure
- Jungle Cruise
- Tarzan's Treehouse
- Walt Disney's Enchanted Tiki Room

History

On opening day in 1955, Adventureland was almost entirely centered around the Jungle Cruise attraction. At that time, the animatronic animals, carefully engineered scenery, and thoroughly detailed theming struck new ground in defining what a theme park attraction could be.

Over the years, several additional features were added to the Adventureland landscape, but the area's theming has remained relatively consistent. Modern franchises such as Tarzan and Indiana Jones have found their place among the wilderness, and the land's overall focus has shifted from the Jungle Cruise to the wildly popular Indiana Jones Adventure, but at heart Adventureland remains a classic vision of exotic exploration and discovery.

Indiana Jones Adventure

About the Attraction

Indiana Jones Adventure: Temple of the Forbidden Eye is a fast-paced, indoor attraction that uses Jeep-like Enhanced Motion Vehicles to transport passengers through a dark ride based on the popular movie franchise. The attraction opened in 1995, and was built in the location previously occupied by the "Eeyore" parking lot.

Behind the Scenes

- The Enhanced Motion Vehicles incorporate hydraulic lifts that create the tilting and shaking motions of the ride's turbulent journey.
- Throughout the ride Indiana Jones is not played by Harrison Ford, as in the movies, but rather by David Temple, a voiceover specialist who studied Harrison Ford's performances in order to mimic his speech.
- The "three doors" at the beginning of the ride are an illusion. There is only one door and one path, but the room rotates and the lights change to give the impression of multiple options.

Indiana Jones Adventure

- Near the end of the ride, when the giant boulder appears to roll toward the car, the boulder is spinning more or less in place. The car and the room's walls both move forward to give the illusion of an approaching boulder and a car that idles, reverses, and finally charges forward.

Things to Look For

- While not easy to spot due to the darkness, there is an "Eeyore" parking sign in the rafters of the projector room in the queue. This is in recognition of the "Eeyore" parking lot that the ride replaced.
- The letters on the walls of the queue are written in the fictitious language Marabic, and correspond directly to English letters. Look at them closely.
- In the spike room of the queue, there is a loose bamboo support pole that responds when shaken.

Quick Facts

- Opened: March 3, 1995
- Vehicle type: Enhanced motion vehicle in the style of a troop transport
- Vehicle capacity: 12
- Soundtrack: Re-recorded adaptation of original John Williams scores

Jungle Cruise

About the Attraction

The Jungle Cruise was one of the original attractions featured at Disneyland's opening. It consists of a guided journey through four tree-covered "rivers" featuring animals and thematic scenes loosely based on the movie *The African Queen* (1951).

Behind the Scenes

- The Jungle Cruise spiel has taken on an identity all its own over the years. While each river guide is given a standard set of jokes to crack and comments to make, many choose to improvise portions of the cruise.
- It is rumored that the Jungle Cruise was the first ride to prompt Walt Disney's idea of "plussing" (continuously adding to an attraction to maintain interest in it). He reportedly struck upon the idea after hearing a family decide not to take the cruise because they had done so on a previous visit.
- Walt originally considered the possibility of keeping live animals along the route of the Jungle Cruise, but ran into difficulties with this plan.

Jungle Cruise

Things to Look For

- Each guide carries a .38 caliber Smith & Wesson handgun, very much a real gun, although it is loaded with blanks. Firing these blanks can either be a method of entertaining passengers or a signal to the ride foreman that the boat is stuck or having a mechanical failure, depending upon the manner in which they are fired.
- While it is rare for the general public to see them, leeches have been found throughout the Jungle Cruise waters, most likely imported along with the exotic plants used along the ride.
- During the ambushed-by-natives portion of the trip, if the jungle is quiet enough, it is possible to hear one of the natives distinctly say "I love disco" over the gibberish that the others are shouting.

Quick Facts

- Opened: July 17, 1955 (opened with Disneyland Park)
- Area: 217,800 sq. ft.
- Boats on water: 12
- Ride duration: Approximately 9 minutes
- Sections: Zambezi, Irrawaddy, Schweitzer Falls, and the Congo

Tarzan's Treehouse

About the Attraction

A giant treehouse containing scenes and interactive elements adapted from the movie *Tarzan*, Tarzan's Treehouse replaced the Swiss Family Treehouse in 1999 as Disney Imagineers re-worked the attraction's content to represent the 1999 movie *Tarzan,* as opposed to the 1960 movie *Swiss Family Robinson*.

Behind the Scenes

- The foliage of the artificial tree primarily consists of hundreds of thousands of vinyl leaves, which were replaced in 1999 during the makeover, although one branch from the original tree remains.
- The tree upon which the treehouse rests was modeled after a Moreton Bay Fig tree, known for the roots that drop down from its branches.

Things to Look For

- Look for the warning "mind thy head" on one of the first branches. This is in tribute to an identical sign in the original treehouse.

Tarzan's Treehouse

- The gramophone near the base camp of the tree-house plays the song "Swisskapolka" from the *Swiss Family Robinson* film as a tribute to the attraction's past identity. The song was remixed by Imagineer Glenn Barker to give it the crackles and skips of a 78 rpm gramophone record.
- In the cooking area, there is a stove with a teapot on it. Pump the bellows near the stove to see it come to life and to watch the teapot react as though it is being heated.
- Close to the stove, on a crate near the hanging pans, are Mrs. Potts and Chip from the movie *Beauty and the Beast*.
- There are weighted-down ropes as you come out of the treehouse that, when pulled forcefully, play one of several sound effects.

Quick Facts

- **Opened originally: November 18, 1962**
- **Tarzan version opened: June 23, 1999**
- **Originally named: "The Swiss Family Tree House"**
- **Scientific name of tree:** *Disneyodendron semperflorens Grandis* **(large, always-flowering Disney tree)**

Walt Disney's Enchanted Tiki Room

About the Attraction

The Tiki Room is a Polynesian-styled theater in which animatronic birds host a performance that includes singing flowers, chanting totem poles, and a magical fountain center-piece. All of these ele-ments are combined in a multi-part musical produc-tion centered around the famous "In the Tiki, Tiki, Tiki Room" theme song.

Behind the Scenes

- The Tiki Room was originally intended to be a res-taurant where animatronic birds and automated water features would provide a tropical environ-ment for diners.
- In order to achieve a more realistic look, the Tiki Room birds are covered, with the exception of their chests, in real bird feathers.
- The magic fountain effect is achieved by raising and lowering a vertical clear pipe through which the water flows. As the water splashes down from the top of the pipe, it disguises the pipe's presence to give the illusion of a free-standing water stream.

Walt Disney's Enchanted Tiki Room

Things to Look For

- The drink stand in the Tiki Room waiting area serves the "Dole Whip" soft-serve dessert which, although not a particularly healthy frozen treat, is not widely sold outside of Disneyland and is definitely worth a try, if only for the novelty.
- For a bit of extra fun, ask a Cast Member before the show starts if you or your child can wake up José, the animatronic master of ceremonies. While the task is usually performed by a Cast Member, they often have no problem allowing someone else to do it.
- The fountain base in the middle of the room was initially planned as a drink station when the Tiki Room was slated to open as a restaurant, and components of its original design remain.

Quick Facts

- Opened: June 23, 1963
- Courtyard pre-show length: 10 minutes
- Show length: 16 minutes
- Hosts: José, Michael, Pierre, and Fritz
- Total animatronic performers: 225
- Original sponsor: United Airlines
- Current sponsor: Dole

Critter Country

Critter Country

Attractions

- Davy Crockett's Explorer Canoes
- The Many Adventures of Winnie the Pooh
- Splash Mountain

History

Tucked away behind the Rivers of America, Critter Country is a descendant of the original Indian Village area, where guests could observe and participate in Native American traditions. The area was first renovated to form Bear Country in 1972, which was centered around the Country Bear Jamboree. However, before Splash Mountain was opened in 1989, the land was renamed "Critter Country" to establish the position of Splash Mountain as the area's featured attraction.

In 2003, the Country Bear Jamboree show was replaced with The Many Adventures of Winnie the Pooh, despite a great deal of protest from longtime fans of the Country Bears. However, this renovation has allowed Critter Country to be the center for all things Winnie the Pooh in the park, much to the delight of many younger guests.

Davy Crockett's Explorer Canoes

About the Attraction

The only completely guest-powered ride in Disneyland Park, the Explorer Canoe attraction takes riders on a human-powered trip around Tom Sawyer Island. Two guides accompany the guests on each trip and point out the various sights along the way, in addition to providing paddling instructions.

Behind the Scenes

- This attraction is usually only open when the park is experiencing fairly large crowds, and only when the weather permits.
- The canoes are a favorite for Cast Members looking for a bit of fun during times when the park is closed, and employee canoe races are said to be a fairly common occurrence, especially early in the morning during the summertime.
- Despite their seemingly consistent courses, the Explorer Canoes, along with the Tom Sawyer rafts, are completely free-floating and rely purely on manual steering.

Davy Crockett's Explorer Canoes

- The Cast Member guides often provide a tremendous amount of paddling assistance, doing much more than their fair share (sometimes as much as half of the total work needed) to make up for guests' lack of expertise, so thank your guides with extra enthusiasm!

Things to Look For

- If you're really feeling motivated, try to get the other guests in the boat to paddle as fast and hard as they can, and you might be able to pass the boat in front of you, which adds some competitive fun to the experience.

Quick Facts

- Opened: July 4, 1956
- Originally named: "Indian War Canoes"
- Originally guided by an American Indian Guide
- Re-named: May 19, 1971
- Maximum riders: 20
- Trip time: 5-10 minutes

The Many Adventures of Winnie the Pooh

About the Attraction

The Many Adventures of Winnie the Pooh is a dark ride attraction that takes guests through a number of scenes based on the animated film of the same name. The ride replaced the classic Country Bear Jamboree attraction, a change that was met with great protest among many Disneyland patrons. The attraction has relatively short wait times, and is geared toward a younger audience.

Behind the Scenes

- Much of the protest over the replacement of the Country Bear Jamboree centered around criticism of the decisions of the managers at the time, Cynthia Harris and Paul Pressler, who oversaw Disneyland operations from 1997 to 2003. While not everyone is in agreement over the nature of their legacy, the general sentiment is that Harris and Pressler shifted the park's emphasis from quality design and Imagineering to profit margins and merchandising.

The Many Adventures of Winnie the Pooh

Things to Look For

- As you exit the Heffalumps and Woozles area, look behind you and you will see three trophy animal heads over an archway. These are Max (a buck), Buff (a buffalo), and Melvin (a moose) from the Country Bear Jamboree attraction that was replaced by Winnie the Pooh.
- The Pooh Corner shop is one of several shops across Disneyland that sells fresh fudge, made on-site at the park. They offer a rotating "fudge of the month" which corresponds to the season (for example, October's fudge is traditionally pumpkin-flavored), which is always interesting to try.

Quick Facts

- Opened: April 11, 2003
- Replaced: Country Bear Jamboree
- Estimated construction budget: $30 million
- Vehicle type: "Hunny Beehive"
- Vehicle capacity: 6
- Recommended seating in vehicle: First two rows

Splash Mountain

About the Attraction

One of Disneyland's most popular attractions, Splash Mountain is famous for its 52.5-foot watery plunge down a 47-degree incline. The ride as a whole is centered around the story in *Song of the South*, a 1946 film about Br'er Rabbit's adventures.

Behind the Scenes

- The majority of the Splash Mountain ride takes place in a warehouse structure outside of the park, with the transitions between scenes inside the mountain, and scenes inside the warehouse being cleverly disguised.
- As the logs reach the peak for the major drop, hidden wheels on their bases make contact with a guide track to ensure that the drop is smooth and that the logs do not stray from the inclined track.
- At the bottom of the major drop, pressurized water jets add extra intensity to the splash in order to increase the effect.

Splash Mountain

- The pictures taken by the camera during the major drop are screened for appropriateness by Cast Members as they are taken, and pictures judged to be inappropriate are removed from the system and are not available for purchase.

Things to Look For

- Before one of the small drops, there is a cave labeled as the home of Br'er Bear. You should be able to hear a snoring sound coming from inside the cave. This snoring is the same track that was played in the sleeping bear cave (Rufus' cave) that used to be located where Splash Mountain is now.
- After the major drop, the logs pass briefly into the Rivers of America before floating back into Splash Mountain.

Quick Facts

- Opened: July 17, 1989
- Ride length: 12 minutes
- Angle of major drop: 47°
- Max speed: 40 mph
- Soundtrack: "How Do You Do?," "Ev'rybody Has a Laughing Place," "Burrow's Lament," and "Zip-A-Dee-Doo-Dah"

Fantasyland

Attractions

- Alice in Wonderland
- Casey Jr. Circus Train
- Dumbo the Flying Elephant
- "It's a Small World"
- King Arthur Carrousel
- Mad Tea Party
- Matterhorn Bobsleds
- Mr. Toad's Wild Ride
- Peter Pan's Flight
- Pinocchio's Daring Journey
- Sleeping Beauty Castle
- Snow White's Scary Adventures
- Storybook Land Canal Boats

History

Opening with the park in 1955, Fantasyland is at the very center of Disneyland's historic identity. It was in the stylized buildings lining Fantasyland's walkways that Walt Disney engineered the transitions of major classic Disney franchises from the film world to physical existence within Disneyland. The idea of the "dark ride," a moving vehicle attraction that tells a story, came to fruition within the bounds of Fantasyland under Walt's supervision and has been an integral part of Disneyland design ever since.

Alice in Wonderland

About the Attraction

Alice in Wonderland is a dark ride attraction that more or less follows the various scenes in the movie of the same name. It was the second attraction in Disneyland to be based on the movie *Alice in Wonderland*, the first being the Mad Tea Party.

Behind the Scenes

- The voice of Alice in the ride is that of Kathryn Beaumont, the same actress that voiced the character in the 1951 Disney film.
- The attraction is located within the second floor of the Mr. Toad's Wild Ride building, and as a result the majority of the track is above ground level. This becomes evident after the "escape from the Queen" scene, as riders are taken outside of the building and find themselves on the second level.
- Before a 1980's renovation, the ride followed the movie chronologically, but after the renovation the Unbirthday/Tea Party scene was relocated to the end of the ride to give the attraction more of a grand finish.

Alice in Wonderland

Things to Look For

- Between Alice in Wonderland and the Matterhorn there is a small cave in the rock along the path where the Cheshire Cat can be found.
- At the beginning of the ride, near the White Rabbit's portrait, look at the shelf on the left to see some books with odd titles.
- There used to be a caterpillar sitting on top of the mushroom where the "A Very Merry Unbirthday to You" book is placed, but he was relocated. If you look carefully when you are riding through the second-story outdoor track area, you can see that only the caterpillar's shoes remain on the mushroom cap.

Quick Facts

- Opened: June, 1958
- Renovated: 1983-1984
- Vehicle type: Colored caterpillar
- Vehicle capacity: 4
- Ride length: Approximately 3 minutes
- Closed: During rainfall, due to slippery tracks

Casey Jr. Circus Train

About the Attraction

Based on the train from the film *Dumbo* (1941), the Casey Jr. Circus Train travels through the Storybook Land area of Fantasyland, allowing guests to observe the miniature landscapes, but in a faster manner than on the canal boats. Guests can choose to ride on a variety of circus-style train cars, including transport cars for monkeys and other animals.

Behind the Scenes

- The sleigh-style train cars were adapted from the King Arthur Carrousel nearby when that attraction replaced some of its sleighs with horses early in its existence. Not wanting to discard the equipment, Imagineers fitted the sleighs with wheels and moved them across Fantasyland to be a part of the Casey Jr. train.
- The actual pulling of the circus train is done not by the obvious engine in front, but rather by the second, whistling music car which has a combustion engine hidden within it.

Casey Jr. Circus Train

Things to Look For

- Listen to hear Casey say, in his subtle whistle voice, "I think I can, I think I can" in the style of *The Little Engine that Could* as he climbs the hill.
- The scale of the structures and landscaping throughout Storybook Land is 1 inch to 1 foot. Keep an eye out for miniaturized landmarks from Disney films, but be sure to ride the Storybook Land Canal Boats for a closer and more detailed look at the models and landscaping.
- See the article on the Storybook Land Canal Boats for more information on Storybook Land as a whole.

Quick Facts

- Opened: July 17, 1955 (opened with Disneyland Park)
- Ride length: Approximately 3 minutes
- Train car types: Engine, music car, sleighs, wild animal cages, caboose
- Recommended seating: Back of caboose

Dumbo the Flying Elephant

About the Attraction

Dumbo the Flying Elephant is based on the 1941 movie *Dumbo*, and incorporates rideable, flying elephants that orbit around a central hub. Guests can choose how high their elephant flies by operating a lever control, adding to the ride's excitement factor among young park-goers and giving the attraction a consistently long line.

Behind the Scenes

- The original design for the attraction featured ten "Pink Elephants on Parade," modeled after the elephants in Timothy Mouse and Dumbo's hallucination in *Dumbo*. Walt decided against this design, not wanting the ride to mirror the alcohol-induced hallucination of the film, and opted to have all of the elephants be Dumbo look-alikes.
- In 1957, former President and Democrat Harry Truman took a trip to Disneyland, but opted not to ride Dumbo the Flying Elephant out of concern that he would be identified with elephants, the symbol of the Republican party.

Dumbo the Flying Elephant

Things to Look For

- Timothy Mouse can be seen standing on top of the ride's central pillar. He originally held a training whip, but this was changed to the magic feather from the film, although the feather was recently replaced so that he is once again holding a whip.
- The music for the ride (and a large portion of Fantasyland) is often provided by the nearby calliope, an instrument built in 1915.
- Take a look at the Dumbo topiaries in the planters around the ride. They are extremely detailed and excellent examples of the carefully maintained landscape design throughout the park.

Quick Facts

- Opened: Late 1955
- Vehicle type: Dumbo look-alike
- Number of vehicles: 16
- Ride length: Approximately 1.5 minutes
- Rotates: Counterclockwise
- Hosted by: Timothy Mouse

"It's a Small World"

About the Attraction

With one of the catchiest theme songs in all of Disneyland, "It's a Small World" promotes world peace by incorporating groups of children representing various regions of the globe, all singing the annoyingly catchy tune. Note: As of this writing, "Small World" is undergoing major renovations.

Behind the Scenes

- As explained by "It's a Small World" composers The Sherman Brothers, one important element to the song's catchiness is that throughout the verse and chorus, the same chords can be played but with different melodies, giving it a "repetitive, yet varied pattern" according to them.

Things to Look For

- In The Finale Room, a clown riding in a hot air balloon is the only figure in the ride known to be frowning (aside from the parents who are dragged on it for the tenth time by their kids).

"It's a Small World"

- The sequences of the rooms and the languages in which the song is sung are as follows: The Hello Room, Scandinavia (Swedish), Europe (German, English, Dutch, French, Italian), Asia (Japanese), Africa (English with drum accompaniment), South America (Spanish), South Seas (merfolk speak, Polynesian languages), New Guinea, The Finale Room (English), and The Goodbye Room.
- The boat storage and service area has an entrance right before the South America scene and an exit right after it. If you look closely, you will see curtain-like objects on the side of the boat canal covering both the entrance and exit. A Cast Member will pull the empty boats through here at the end of the day.

Quick Facts

- **Opened: May 28, 1966**
- **Originally designed for: 1964 World's Fair in New York City**
- **Vehicle type: Boat**
- **Vehicle capacity: 20**
- **Ride length: Approximately 14 minutes**
- **Animatronics: >300**

King Arthur Carrousel

About the Attraction

The King Arthur Carrousel was included in the park by Walt Disney because he believed that a carousel was an essential element in the theme park experience. It is an authentic nineteenth century antique carousel that has been adapted to the theme from the movie *The Sword in the Stone* (1963).

Behind the Scenes

- The carousel was operated at Sunnyside Amusement Park in Toronto, Canada before being relocated in 1954 to Disneyland where it received significant renovations.
- Each horse on the carousel was hand-carved in the nineteenth century, and all of the horses are unique.
- Because Walt wanted the carousel to contain horses exclusively, the sleighs that were originally a part of the carousel were re-purposed as train cars for the Casey Jr. Circus Train.

King Arthur Carrousel

- Repainting each horse requires as many as 40 hours of labor, so a rotating repainting cycle is used, with each horse receiving a fresh paint job about every two years.

Things to Look For

- The painted panels that run along the top of the carrousel depict scenes from the story of Sleeping Beauty.
- The horse named Jingles is often considered to be the lead horse on the carousel. She is easy to spot, as she is covered in strings of bells. She was also painted gold for the Disneyland 50th anniversary celebration.

Quick Facts

- Opened: July 17, 1955 (opened with Disney-land Park)
- Number of horses: 72
- Ride length: Approximately 2 minutes (8 revolutions)
- Originally built: 1875
- Dramatic refurbishment: 2002-2003

Mad Tea Party

About the Attraction

Based on the 1951 film *Alice in Wonderland*, the Mad Tea Party centers around the "Unbirthday" scene and incorporates numerous spinning teacups in which guests can sit. Each teacup is controlled by the people sitting in it, so guests are able to choose how intense they want the ride to be. This ride can be extremely nauseating and many guests over the years have overestimated their ability to resist motion sickness, resulting in some very speedy trips to the nearest trash can.

Behind the Scenes

- In 2004 the teacups were adjusted to spin noticeably slower. While this was officially attributed to a routine refurbishment, it is rumored that a previous incident of a rider falling out of one of the cups may have contributed to the decision to restrict their spinning speeds. A series of inquiries to California authorities by Disneyland patrons confirmed that the change was not influenced by state or local regulation, but rather by Disneyland management.

Mad Tea Party

Things to Look For

- For a bit of extra fun, ask the ride operator if they will declare a competition to see which group can spin their cup the fastest. They will often oblige, and it can add some competitive spirit to the ride.
- The orange diamond cup and the purple cup are usually considered to be the fastest spinning cups on the ride, although everyone has their own theory on which cup to choose for the best spin, so you might want to ask the ride operator which cups are riding the fastest currently.
- Once in a while, characters from *Alice in Wonderland* will ride along with guests in teacups that have empty spaces.

Quick Facts

- Opened: July 17, 1955 (opened with Disneyland Park)
- Vehicle type: Teacup
- Vehicles: 18
- Ride length: Approximately 1.5 minutes
- Closed: During rainfall, due to slippery turntables

Matterhorn Bobsleds

About the Attraction

Modeled after an actual mountain in the Swiss Alps, Disneyland's Matterhorn was built to 1/100 scale of the approximately 14,000 ft. peak in the Alps. The Matterhorn at Disneyland houses a bobsled-based steel roller coaster with two separate tracks that intertwine throughout the mountain.

Behind the Scenes

- In addition to being an important element of Disneyland's history, the Matterhorn Bobsleds represent an important milestone in roller coaster design. The Matterhorn was the first operating steel roller coaster in the world, with nylon wheels rolling along steel tube rails to give it a more versatile and elegant design than was previously possible.
- While often dismissed as a rumor, there is indeed a basketball court inside the Matterhorn. Constructed as a way for Cast Members climbing the mountain to pass the time, the roughly-assembled half-court occupies a break room near the top of the Matterhorn.

Matterhorn Bobsleds

Things to Look For

- Every once in a while, Cast Members dressed as Swiss mountain climbers will scale the peak of the Matterhorn, sometimes joined by various Disney characters.
- There is a Yeti footprint on the ground among the flowers near the benches across from the Matterhorn queue.
- In the dark tunnel where only the red monster eyes are visible, look up and you might catch a glimpse of some of the Matterhorn's internal framework and supports.
- The Matterhorn's Yeti is nicknamed "Harold" by Cast Members. For a bit of fun, try asking a Cast Member how Harold is doing today.

Quick Facts

- Opened: June 14, 1959
- Vehicle type: 4-person bobsled
- Mountain height: 147 ft.
- Highest point on track: 80 ft.
- Ride length: Approximately 2.25 minutes
- Bobsled max speed: 27 mph

Mr. Toad's Wild Ride

About the Attraction

Mr. Toad's Wild Ride is a dark ride attraction that incorporates elements of the *Wind in the Willows* segment of the 1949 film *The Adventures of Ichabod and Mr. Toad*. The ride takes guests through a series of scenes, including a crash through a fireplace, a collision with an oncoming train, and a journey through "The Inferno Room."

Behind the Scenes

- The attraction is located in the same building as Alice in Wonderland, although Mr. Toad's Wild Ride takes place primarily on the first floor and Alice in Wonderland largely occupies the second.
- Throughout the ride, Mr. Toad himself is only seen as a statue and in pictures because the idea is that the riders should assume the role of the main character (Mr. Toad) and experience events through his eyes. This used to be the model for most of the Fantasyland dark rides, but the policy changed after guests complained that the main characters were not present in their own rides.

Mr. Toad's Wild Ride

Things to Look For

- Written on the shield above the entrance to the attraction is the motto "Toadi Acceleratio Semper Absurda," translating roughly to "Speeding with Toad is Always Absurd."
- In the window to the left of the entrance is a statue of Mr. Toad with his arms behind his back. This statue originally had him extending a hand up and out, but was likely changed due to the common tendency of guests to place various items between his fingers.
- After you exit Winky's pub, look at the upstairs windows of the buildings in the town. In one of them there is a silhouette of detective Sherlock Holmes.

Quick Facts

- Opened: July 17, 1955 (opened with Disneyland Park)
- Vehicle type: Horseless carriage
- Ride length: 2 minutes
- Car names: Mr. Toad, Mole, Badger, Cyril, Weasel, Winky, Ratty

Peter Pan's Flight

About the Attraction

Based on the 1953 film *Peter Pan*, the attraction uses vehicles mounted on overhead tracks rather than tracks laid on the floor in order to give riders the sensation of flight. The ride takes guests on a flying tour over landmarks in both London and Neverland, and incorporates a variety of scenes from the movie *Peter Pan*.

Behind the Scenes

- The effect of cars moving through the streets of London is achieved by pulling strands of reflective paint dots through the town model.
- The cloud effect below you in the London fly-by is formed from plastic-like material that flows gently across the scene.
- The volcano effect in the Neverland scene is created by blowing beads out of the artificial volcano and shining orange light up through them.

Peter Pan's Flight

Things to Look For

- While in the queue, look at the upper-story window of the Snow White attraction. Every once in a while, the Evil Queen will peek out of it and you can get a great view from here.
- The stacked blocks in the Darling nursery spell the words "Disney" (when read from bottom to top) and "PPan."
- Just as you pass through the nursery window, look down the side of the house and you will see the Darling family's dog, Nana.
- When flying over London, you will see that Big Ben stands on its own amidst the cityscape. In reality, Big Ben is a part of the House of Parliament building.

Quick Facts

- Opened: July 17, 1955 (opened with Disneyland Park)
- Vehicle type: Flying galleon
- Vehicle seating: 2 adults and 1 child or equivalent
- Ride length: Approximately 2 minutes

Pinocchio's Daring Journey

About the Attraction

Based on the 1940 film *Pinocchio*, Pinocchio's Daring Journey is a dark ride that follows the events of Pinocchio's quest to become a real boy. The ride incorporates scenes such as Stromboli's circus and Pleasure Island that follow the plot of the film, and makes use of a variety of interesting visual effects.

Behind the Scenes

- Revolutionary at the time of the ride's introduction, holographic techniques (such as the Pepper's ghost effect), are used to depict transparent objects and a morphing sequence. Plate glass is placed between two rooms that are identical except for the object that will appear/disappear or change its shape. The lighting is then shifted between the rooms so that viewers see a transition between the arrangement of objects in the first room and that of the second.

Pinocchio's Daring Journey

- Also revolutionary at the time, fiber optic effects are prominent throughout the ride, and are used to create the effect of sparkling stars among other things.

Things to Look For

- The weathervane on the roof of the building that encloses the attraction forms a whale shape that corresponds to the silhouette of Monstro from the film, depicted here in pursuit of a school of fish.
- Just as you are leaving the Blue Fairy scene, you may have an opportunity to catch a quick glimpse of the room on the other side of the plate glass, in which the tangible Blue Fairy is located for use in the Pepper's ghost effect.

Quick Facts

- Opened: May 23, 1983
- Ride length: Approximately 3 minutes
- Vehicle seating: 4 guests per car in 2 rows
- Replaced: Fantasyland Theater
- Vehicle carvings: Jiminy Cricket, Cleo, and Figaro

Sleeping Beauty Castle

About the Attraction

Sleeping Beauty Castle is the centerpiece of Disneyland Park and an immensely important landmark throughout Disneyland's history. It has also grown to become a widely recognized symbol  for the Walt Disney Company itself, and is used in numerous Disney-related logos and designs.

Behind the Scenes

- When designing Sleeping Beauty Castle, Walt Disney was inspired by Neuschwanstein Castle in Bavaria, and the connection between the two is immediately evident in the picture comparison above (Neuschwanstein is pictured on the right).
- Guests used to be able to walk up into a part of the castle and view an animatronic depiction of the Sleeping Beauty story. However, this attraction was closed in 2001.
- The drawbridge in front of the castle is fully functional, but is only raised and lowered on very rare occasions. You can see some of the mechanisms used for raising it if you look nearby in the castle.

Sleeping Beauty Castle

- The castle's architecture uses forced perspective to achieve the effect of greater height. Going up each turret, the castle's stones get smaller and smaller.

Things to Look For

- The Disney family crest can be seen above the entrance to Sleeping Beauty Castle, just after crossing the drawbridge.
- The "gargoyles" on Sleeping Beauty Castle are actually shaped like harmless, furry squirrels.
- After crossing the bridge and going through the castle, look for a golden spike in the ground. Many reports say that this used to mark the center of Disneyland, although the park's many changes over the years have shifted its exact geographical center to a different location.

Quick Facts

- Opened: July 17, 1955 (opened with Disneyland Park)
- Height: 77 feet
- Corresponds with: *Sleeping Beauty* (1959)
- Spire plating: 22-karat gold

Snow White's Scary Adventures

About the Attraction

Snow White's Scary Adventures is one of the original Fantasyland dark rides, and is based on the 1937 film *Snow White and the Seven Dwarfs*. It incorporates numerous scenes from the movie and roughly follows the same plot. Although the title suggests otherwise, the ride is quite tame.

Behind the Scenes

- Originally, Snow White was nowhere to be seen within the attraction itself. This was because the ride was designed to put guests in the main character's shoes, like many of the other Fantasyland dark rides at the time. However, Snow White was added during a Fantasyland renovation in 1983 in response to numerous guests' complaints that Snow White wasn't in her own ride.
- Since 1983, the voice of Snow White throughout the ride has been that of Adriana Caselotti, who voiced Snow White in the 1937 film.

Snow White's Scary Adventures

- In one scene, the Queen offers an apple to guests as she holds it in her outstretched hand. Guests would often accept her offer and grab this apple as a souvenir, so the physical apple was replaced with a hologram to prevent theft.

Things to Look For

- Be sure to check the window above the entrance to the ride (pictured on the previous page) while you are waiting in line. Every once in a while the Evil Queen will look out through the curtains.

Quick Facts

- Opened: July 17, 1955 (opened with Disney-land Park)
- Vehicle type: Dwarfs' mine cars
- Vehicle capacity: 4
- Vehicles named after the Seven Dwarfs (Bashful, Doc, Dopey, Grumpy, Happy, Sleepy, and Sneezy)

Storybook Land Canal Boats

About the Attraction

The Canal Boats feature a gentle and slow-paced ride through the miniature landscapes of Storybook Land. While not based on any particular Disney film or production, the scenes in Storybook Land draw from a variety of well-known Disney titles.

Behind the Scenes

- The ride was originally titled "Canal Boats of the World" and was intended to be a journey through miniature re-creations of world landmarks.
- The original construction of the ride faced numerous problems including noisy and unreliable outboard gas motors and a consistent lack of landscaping that led to the unfortunate nickname "The Mud Bank Ride."
- The attraction was redone in mid-1956, taking on its present form and title, with completed landscaping and reliable electric motors that run much more quietly and efficiently than gas ones.

Storybook Land Canal Boats

- The buildings and landscaping (including the incredible collection of bonsai plant life) in Storybook Land are on a scale of 1 inch to 1 foot.

Things to Look For

- When you pass by the miniature Alpine village, notice how the scene is oriented in such a way that the miniature Alps are aligned with Matterhorn mountain in the distance.
- Sometimes the guide will allow kids to sit on the front of the boat, and might designate these kids as the boat's "whale watchers."
- If you catch him at the right time, Monstro the whale will slowly open and close his eyes and squirt bursts of water out of his blowhole every once in a while.

Quick Facts

- Opened: July 17, 1955 (opened with Disneyland Park)
- Vehicle type: Small boat
- Vehicle capacity: 14
- Vehicles in use: 13
- Ride length: Approximately 5 minutes

Frontierland

Frontierland

Attractions

- Big Thunder Mountain Railroad
- Mark Twain Riverboat
- Pirate's Lair at Tom Sawyer Island
- Sailing Ship Columbia

History

Frontierland is a romantic image of America in the Old West as Walt Disney envisioned it, filled with abandoned mines, covered wagons, and stage-coaches. Opening with Disneyland Park in 1955, Frontierland was focused around the central element of the Rivers of America. The original concept behind the land was that it would be a place to experience wide-open wilderness and navigate the trails of untouched natural landscape.

Original attractions such as pack mules and hiking trails created a scene of undeveloped Western territory. However, this image of Frontierland did not remain for long. Over the years, the land transformed from a sparsely populated wilderness to a bustling town of the Old West.

Big Thunder Mountain Railroad

About the Attraction

The Big Thunder Mountain Railroad replaced the Mine Train through Nature's Wonderland, but kept the idea of a mine train tour, this time with the idea that the mine train would create the impression of being wild and out of control.

Behind the Scenes

- The inspiration for the ride's appearance came from the rock formations in Bryce Canyon National Park, Utah.
- The train can move as much as 5 mph faster on warm afternoons because the sun heats the grease used to lubricate each car's moving parts.
- Well-known among Cast Members and frequent riders is the "Goat Trick" where, by keeping your eye focused on the dynamite-chewing goat (pictured above) at the top of the second hill, you can increase the apparent intensity of the spiral drop.

Big Thunder Mountain Railroad

Things to Look For

- Bits and pieces from the Mine Train through Nature's Wonderland still exist as parts of Thunder Mountain. The first cave that the train enters contains crystal formations and pools in the style of those featured in the Rainbow Caverns portion of the Mine Train through Nature's Wonderland.
- The entrance to the first mine shaft (with the crystal formations) is marked by a right-side-up horseshoe, but the entrance to the mine shaft with the unsteady boulders toward the end of the ride is marked by an upside-down horseshoe, a symbol of bad luck.
- The splash at the end of the ride is actually created not by the train hitting the pool of water, but by a series of pipes that spray the water out from under the tracks at the moment the train goes over them.

Quick Facts

- Opened: September 2, 1979
- Vehicle type: Mine train
- Vehicle capacity: 30
- Vehicles in use: 5 at a time
- Ride length: Approximately 3 minutes
- Mountain peak height: 104 ft.

Mark Twain Riverboat

About the Attraction

Every 25 minutes, the Mark Twain Riverboat begins its tour around the Rivers of America, giving guests an authentic stern-wheel steamboat experience narrated by both Thurl Ravenscroft (a  common voice in Disneyland attractions, and the voice of Kellogg's Tony the Tiger for over fifty years) and another actor playing the role of Mark Twain.

Behind the Scenes

- The riverboat travels along an I-beam track set under the water, so the pilot and boiler engineer do not have control over the boat's direction and must avoid other river traffic by speeding up and slowing down appropriately. The pilot acts as a lookout and signals to the boiler engineer when to speed up and slow down.
- In its first days of operation, the riverboat operators were unsure as to its maximum capacity, and would often allow as many as 500 people to board the boat. This caused problems as the deck would be pushed down to just inches above the water.

Mark Twain Riverboat

- Less than a week before Disneyland opened in 1955, Walt and Lillian Disney celebrated their 30th wedding anniversary aboard the Mark Twain, with additional accommodations in the Golden Horse-shoe theater.

Things to Look For

- When you are boarding the Mark Twain, you can ask a Cast Member if it would be possible for you to ride with the pilot at the top of the boat. The pilot often allows small groups of people to ride along in the wheelhouse and work some of the signals. It makes for a memorable experience, especially for younger guests, and you will be able to sign the guest-book and receive a certificate.

Quick Facts

- Opened: July 17, 1955 (opened with Disneyland Park)
- Ride length: Approximately 12 minutes
- Ride capacity: 300
- Length of ship's hull: 105 ft.
- Engine: diesel-powered boiler

Pirate's Lair on Tom Sawyer Island

About the Attraction

Tom Sawyer Island has been overrun by pirates in this update to the classic attraction in the middle of the Rivers of America. The only way for guests to reach the island is to take a raft across the river, and once on the island there are plenty of pirate-related activities in which to partake.

Behind the Scenes

- Tom Sawyer Island is the only attraction in Disneyland that was single-handedly designed by Walt Disney himself.
- The first time the Rivers of America were filled with water, they drained almost immediately as water seeped out into the soil. Lining the Rivers with clay solved this problem and the second filling effort was successful.
- Guests were originally able to fish in the waters around the island, but this activity was soon discontinued as caught fish would end up discarded throughout the park.

Pirate's Lair on Tom Sawyer Island

- The rafts to the island do not follow any set track and depend upon the pilots to steer them along a fairly consistent path.

Things to Look For

- There is a hidden area beneath Lafitte's Tavern where many technical components for the Fantasmic! show are located.
- The hand and eye in the treasure trove section of Dead Man's Grotto, as well as the voices that accompany them, are those of Pintel and Ragetti, the pirates who provide comic relief in the *Pirates of the Caribbean* films.

Quick Facts

- Original Tom Sawyer Island opened: June 16, 1956
- Pirate's Lair update opened: May 25, 2007
- Rafts in use: 2 at a time
- Avg. raft capacity: 55
- Raft names: "Anne Bonney" and "Blackbeard" after the famous pirates

Sailing Ship Columbia

About the Attraction

The Sailing Ship Columbia offers a similar tour of the Rivers of America as the Mark Twain Riverboat, but is authentically styled as a full-scale replica of an eighteenth century trading ship.

Behind the Scenes

- The Sailing Ship Columbia is modeled after the Columbia Rediviva, the first American ship to circumnavigate the globe.
- The Sailing Ship Columbia has one of the more prominent Disneyland injury accidents associated with it. On December 24, 1998 a husband and wife were both struck by a cleat that was improperly secured to the Columbia's dock, resulting in the death of the husband. This incident was due to both human and mechanical error, and caused widespread investigation into theme park safety regulations and monitoring.
- The Columbia follows the same underwater track as the Mark Twain, and its crew has a similar lack of control over the direction in which the ship sails.

Sailing Ship Columbia

- When the ship was nearing completion, Walt Disney learned that it was tradition to place a silver dollar under a sailing ship's masts and did so personally before the Columbia's masts were set.

Things to Look For

- The sailing songs that play on the Columbia throughout its voyage include *Blow the Man Down*, *Clear the Track*, *One More Day*, *Rolling Home*, and *Song of the Fishes*.
- Below deck is a recreation of the typical quarters for a crew in the late eighteenth century, an exhibit that was added to the Sailing Ship Columbia in 1964.

Quick Facts

- **Opened: June 14, 1958**
- **Ride length: Approximately 12 minutes**
- **Ride capacity: 300**
- **Length of ship's hull: 83.5 ft.**
- **Mast height: 84 ft.**
- **Operates: On days with large crowds and during the Mark Twain's downtime**

Main Street, U.S.A.

Main Street, U.S.A.

Attractions

- Disneyland Railroad
- Main Street Vehicles: Fire Engine, Horse-Drawn Streetcar, Horseless Carriage, and Omnibus

History

Modeled after Walt Disney's hometown of Marceline, Missouri, Main Street, U.S.A. is a vision of American city life in the early 20th century, when Walt was a child. The land has many of the features of a typical American town, including a city hall, a fire department, and a bank. It is perhaps most impressive at night, when the electrical excitement of an age of newfound lighting technology is reflected brilliantly by the glowing buildings on either side of the main thoroughfare.

Main Street, U.S.A. is also home to one of the biggest tributes to many of the people who made Disneyland possible. Looking closely at the windows of almost every building on Main Street, one can see the names of dozens of individuals who contributed substantial time and effort to the betterment of Disneyland. In effect, the windows of Main Street have become a screen for the rolling credits of Disneyland's history.

Disneyland Railroad

About the Attraction

The Disneyland Railroad offers a "grand circle tour" of the park, with stations in Main Street, New Orleans Square, Mickey's Toontown, and Tomorrowland. It originally opened with just two stations but it has expanded over time with the park.

Behind the Scenes

- There is a guideline that instructs all Cast Members near the Disneyland Railroad to stop what they are doing and wave when a train goes by.
- Trains not currently being used are stored in a roundhouse behind "It's a Small World."
- The railroad's water tower is located at the New Orleans Square station, so trains will often make extended stops there as they refill.

Things to Look For

- At 306 ft. long, the Grand Canyon diorama that the train passes through is the longest in the world.
- There is a small bullet hole in the diorama glass.

Disneyland Railroad

- Some of the trains have special seating areas in the engine cab or caboose, and sometimes the Victorian-style VIP observation car, the Lilly Belle, is attached to one of the trains. If you ask a conductor at Main Street station, there is a chance that they will be able to arrange a ride with the engineer at the front of the train, a ride in the caboose, or a rare and very special ride in the exclusive Lilly Belle parlor car. Be advised that these ride options may require that you stay on the railroad for the full "grand circle tour" of the park.
- At the New Orleans Square station, there is a looping telegraph sound that repeats the first two sentences of Walt's Opening Day speech.
- Behind "It's a Small World" the train crosses a small road and a set of crossing signals is activated. These miniature signals were a gift from the Santa Fe Railway, the DLRR's original sponsor.

Quick Facts

- **Opened: July 17, 1955 (opened with Disneyland Park)**
- **Ride length: Approximately 20 minutes**
- **Minimum number of trains running: 2**
- **Original sponsor: Santa Fe Railway**
- **Gauge: 3 ft.**

Main Street Vehicles

About the Attraction

Main Street is filled with a variety of transportation options, including Disneyland Fire Engines, Horse-Drawn Streetcars, Horseless Carriages, and the double-decker Omnibus. While these vehicles are not huge time-savers, they add a fun touch to the ambience of Main Street.

Behind the Scenes

- Main Street itself is based on Marceline, Missouri, where Walt Disney spent his childhood.
- The buildings on Main Street employ forced perspective to appear taller. Each building's second story is on a smaller scale than its first story.
- The horses that pull the streetcars are Belgian and Percheron draft horses, a type of horse that is bred to handle heavy loads.
- Due to the reduced friction of the track that the streetcars follow, each streetcar could easily be pulled by two adult humans.

Main Street Vehicles

- The Omnibus is based on a 1920's era New York City bus and is reported to be capable of traveling as fast as 60 mph.

Things to Look For

- Each of the horses that pull the streetcars has his or her name written on the harness.
- Above the fire station on Main Street is Walt's personal apartment, which is still used on rare occasions. The lamp in the window remains constantly lit in memory of Walt.
- It is often said that when the flags on Main Street are pointing toward the castle, it is about to rain in Disneyland.

Quick Facts

- Horse-drawn streetcars opened: July 17, 1955 (opened with Disneyland Park)
- Horseless carriage opened: May 12, 1956
- Omnibus opened: August 24, 1956
- Fire Engine opened: August 16, 1958

Mickey's Toontown

Mickey's Toontown

Attractions

- Character Houses: Chip 'n Dale Treehouse, Donald's Boat, Mickey's House, and Minnie's House
- Gadget's Go Coaster
- Roger Rabbit's Car Toon Spin

History

Opened in 1993, Mickey's Toontown is the most recent land added to Disneyland Park, and is centered around themes from the 1988 film *Who Framed Roger Rabbit*. The idea behind the land is that live-action humans (in this case, the park guests) can interact directly with cartoons, just as they did in the *Roger Rabbit* film.

While Toontown contains few big feature attractions, it is built around many dozens of small gags and curiosities. Almost every structure in the area has an interactive component, the sum of which gives the impression of an area built in accordance with the wacky logic of cartoons.

Character Houses

About the Attraction

Along with various rides and other attractions, Mickey's Toontown contains an array of Characters' homes including the Chip `n Dale Treehouse, Donald's Boat, Mickey's House, and Minnie's House. Each of these houses offers opportunities to view the character's belongings and even meet the characters in person.

Behind the Scenes

- There can actually be as many as four Mickeys in Mickey's House at a time, each on a different movie set.
- Cast Members will sometimes reward donators to Minnie's wishing well with small tokens of appreciation, such as Disney stickers.
- Like many other structures in Disneyland, the Toontown hills use the technique of forced perspective. The scale of the hills decreases as they get higher, giving them the effect of towering over Toontown.

Character Houses

Things to Look For

- In Mickey's House you can find Mickey's passport in a display case in his living room. Look at it closely and you will see that it has a location stamp for each Disney park around the world.
- Pay attention to the books in both Mickey and Minnie's houses, as many of them have creative and funny titles. It should be noted that interesting titles are a common feature on a large portion of the books used as props throughout Disneyland's attractions.
- Listen for Mickey's voice on Minnie's answering machine.
- Look at the wide variety of cheeses that Minnie keeps in her kitchen.

Quick Facts

- Mickey's Toontown opened: January, 1993
- Movie sets in Mickey's House: *Band Concert*, *Fantasia*, *Steamboat Willie*, and *Thru the Mirror*.
- Mickey's home address: 1 Neighborhood Lane

Gadget's Go Coaster

About the Attraction

Gadget's Go Coaster is based on the Disney television series *Chip 'n Dale Rescue Rangers* and centers around inventor and mechanic Gadget Hackwrench. The attraction is designed for children, and has a theme of improvised construction from salvaged materials including pencils, a comb, a spool, and various building blocks.

Behind the Scenes

- The basis of Gadget's Go Coaster is a standard Vekoma Junior Coaster (also called the Roller Skater), but Disney Imagineers have made extensive modifications to the Vekoma design and have added a wealth of Disney-related touches.
- Gadget's Go Coaster uses a series of spinning "squeeze tires" to climb the lift hill rather than the more conventional chain lift method. This is an element of the Vekoma Junior Coaster design.
- With a line that can reach 30 minutes for only a 45-second ride, this coaster can have one of the poorest time payoffs in the park during peak hours.

Gadget's Go Coaster

- On some versions of the Vekoma Junior Coaster, it is possible to run two trains at once on the track. However, Gadget's Go Coaster is one of the shorter Junior Coaster models (at about 680 ft. long) and thus is limited to one train, making for longer lines.

Things to Look For

- There is a weather vane on the roof of the Go Coaster workshop that is shaped like a silhouette of Gadget, and there is a tree branch growing out of the window below it.
- Gadget's workshop has a series of plans for the various elements of the ride. These are filled with fun little details that make the wait a bit more interesting.

Quick Facts

- Opened: January, 1993 (opened with Mickey's Toontown)
- Vehicles: 1
- Vehicle type: Acorn train
- Vehicle capacity: 16
- Ride length: Approximately 45 seconds
- Max speed: 22 mph

Roger Rabbit's Car Toon Spin

About the Attraction

Similar to the Mad Tea Party in that it allows guests to control the spin of their ride vehicle, Roger Rabbit's Car Toon Spin is an interactive dark ride that incorporates characters and themes from the 1988 movie *Who Framed Roger Rabbit*.

Behind the Scenes

- This attraction does not communicate with the park-wide FastPass network. This means that you can hold FastPasses for Roger Rabbit and another attraction at the same time.
- Roger Rabbit was initially planned to be the central character of a new Hollywoodland, but this idea was eventually merged into Toontown's design.
- The portable hole effect at the end of the ride uses a mirror to reflect a portion of solid wall. The hole is essentially a large box with a circle cut out of it and a mirror on the side that faces toward you as you approach the turn into the hole. When Roger Rabbit deploys the hole, he pushes this box into the wall, hiding the mirror.

Roger Rabbit's Car Toon Spin

Things to Look For

- Look at the license plate numbers on the wall as you enter the building. They represent famous quotes, characters, movies, and other terms that relate to Disney productions.
- At the start of the ride, the DIP cans that the weasels use are actual movie props from *Who Framed Roger Rabbit*.
- Keep an eye out for the Jack-in-the-Boxes stored in the Gag Warehouse. They are based on the faces of Imagineers who worked on the attraction.
- As you come to the end of the ride, the vehicles pass a series of numbered lockers on the right side of the track. Look for one labeled as locker 3.1416 (an approximation of the number Pi).

Quick Facts

- Opened: January 26, 1994
- Vehicle type: Interactive spinning Lenny the Taxi Cab
- Vehicle capacity: 2
- Ride length: Approximately 3.5 minutes
- DIP ingredients: Acetone, Benzene, and Turpentine (all used in paint removers)

New Orleans Square

New Orleans Square

Attractions

- Club 33
- Haunted Mansion
- Pirates of the Caribbean

History

Opened in 1966, New Orleans Square was the first land to be added to Disneyland Park after the park opened in 1955. It replaced the obscure Holidayland, which consisted of outdoor recreational areas and included a circus tent and a baseball field, but lacked Disney theming and proper amenities.

New Orleans Square is based on a romantic vision of the city of New Orleans in the 19th and 20th centuries. The area consists of buildings and decorations in the style of New Orleans' French Quarter, as well as two of Disneyland's most iconic attractions, the Haunted Mansion and Pirates of the Caribbean. Additionally, the streets of New Orleans Square are frequently filled with the performances of jazz and pirate bands to complete the image of historic New Orleans.

Club 33

About the Attraction

Club 33 is an exclusive dining establishment located in the upper stories of the New Orleans Square buildings. It was envisioned by Walt Disney, but completed just after his death. Membership is highly exclusive, and Club 33's waiting list has been reported to be as long as 14 years. The club features fine antique furnishings, a glass elevator, and balcony views of New Orleans square.

Behind the Scenes

- Club 33 serves lunch and dinner, and is equipped to handle large parties and events.
- The club holds a collection of items used in Disney movies, including the telephone booth from *The Happiest Millionaire* and a table from *Mary Poppins.*
- Club 33 also contains an amazing collection of art and photographs relating to Walt and the park.
- Members of the club enjoy numerous benefits, including complimentary admission to the park for themselves and their guests if they plan to dine at Club 33.

Club 33

Things to Look For

- The entrance to Club 33 is next to the entrance to the Blue Bayou restaurant. The door is marked by the street address 33 on a plaque to the right.
- One of the few ways for individuals who are neither members nor guests of members to see the club is on the Walk in Walt's Footsteps tour, which allows participants to view the club's lobby.
- Walt had originally planned for the club to have animatronic animals that would interact with guests. Microphones were placed in the lighting fixtures, so that an actor backstage would be able to hear the guests' conversation and respond through the animatronics. Even though they no longer operate, the microphones' screens can still be seen.

Quick Facts

- Opened: May, 1967
- Corporate membership fee: $25,000 initial and $5,925 annually ($4,375 annually for each additional employee)
- Limited corporate membership fee: $10,000 initial and $4,375 annually (one employee permitted)
- Gold (individual) membership fee: $9,500 initial and $3,175 annually

Haunted Mansion

About the Attraction

The Haunted Mansion incorporates impressive visual effects along with a themed soundtrack and narration. The Ghost Host (voiced by Paul Frees) guides you through a series of spooky scenes as you are carried on a tour of the mansion.

Behind the Scenes

- Most of the attraction is actually enclosed in a massive show building located outside of park grounds. The Stretching Room and Portrait Hall are both used to transport guests under the Disneyland Railroad tracks and into this show building.
- In the Portrait Hall, the busts that turn to follow you are actually indentations in the wall that are lit from behind in order to give the appearance of 3D objects. As you move past the indentations, your perspective on them shifts, causing your brain to conclude that the faces have rotated.
- The Madam Leota effect and other similar effects in the Haunted Mansion are achieved by digitally projecting features onto a faceless model of a head.

Haunted Mansion

- The ballroom scene and other similar visuals use the Pepper's Ghost effect. This involves having two rooms separated by plate glass, with identical set-ups except for what is to appear and disappear. The lighting is then shifted between the rooms to cause these items to appear or become transparent.
- The hitchhiking ghosts are tangible figures behind a one-way mirror. They are carefully lighted so that you see them faintly along with your reflection.

Things to Look For

- There is a spider on the plate glass in the ballroom scene that covers a hole made by a guest's air rifle.
- The second-from-the-left of the graveyard busts that sing Grim Grinning Ghosts is Thurl Raven-scroft, who voiced Frosted Flakes' Tony the Tiger.

Quick Facts

- Opened: August 9, 1969
- Vehicle type: Doom buggy
- Vehicle capacity: 2-3
- Vehicle loading system: Omnimover (non-stop loading of over 2,000 guests per hour)
- Closed: September and January (for Haunted Mansion Holiday conversion)

Pirates of the Caribbean

About the Attraction

A classic Disneyland attraction through-and-through, Pirates of the Caribbean has developed into one of the most successful Disney franchises ever, and it all started with this swashbuckling boat ride through Disneyland's basement.

Behind the Scenes

- Pirates of the Caribbean was originally slated to be a walk-through wax museum attraction, and it was also planned to feature non-humorous, real pirates.
- Over the years, Pirates has faced a great deal of criticism concerning its inclusion of the pirates-chasing-women and bride auction scenes. Although the bride auction scene has remained in place, the chase has been altered dramatically to show women chasing pirates instead.
- There is a skeleton pirate toward the beginning of the ride that appears to be constantly drinking from a bottle. This effect is achieved by rotating a red, corkscrew-like object to give the appearance of flowing liquid.

Pirates of the Caribbean

- The bride auctioneer has been used as a prototype for animatronics development and is a great deal more advanced than the average animatronic.

Things to Look For

- The ironwork above the entrance incorporates the letters 'W' and 'R' for Walt and Roy Disney.
- While drifting through the first stretch of canal after leaving the dock, look up and behind the boat and you will be able to catch a glimpse of the ride's control room.
- Listen for pig squeals and dog barks that go along with the music as you pass by both the pigs in the mud and the dog near the accordion player.

Quick Facts

- Opened: March 18, 1967
- Ride length: Approximately 15 minutes
- Total water: 750,000 gallons across 1,838 ft. of canal
- Show buildings size: 112,826 sq. ft.
- Hourly capacity: Over 3,000 (thanks to efficient loading of large boats)

Tomorrowland

Tomorrowland

Attractions

- Astro Orbitor
- Autopia
- Buzz Lightyear Astro Blasters
- Disneyland Monorail System
- Finding Nemo Submarine Voyage
- Honey, I Shrunk the Audience
- Innoventions
- Space Mountain
- Star Tours

History

Opening with Disneyland Park in 1955, Tomorrowland began with a disappointingly minimal set of attractions. At that time the land was primarily focused around commercial sponsorships, including product showcases for Richfield Oil, Monsanto Chemicals, and other corporations.

Over the years, Tomorrowland has undergone many drastic transitions, including the 1959 addition of the monorail, Submarine Voyage, and Matterhorn (later moved to Fantasyland), the 1967 addition of several new show buildings and theaters, and the 1998 re-theming that introduced Innoventions, the ill-fated Rocket Rods, and other attractions with a new retro-futuristic theme.

Astro Orbitor

About the Attraction

The Astro Orbitor has taken several forms and names over the years, but in its current incarnation it consists of rocket-styled vehicles that orbit a central sculpture. This sculpture has an array of futuristic objects surrounding it that rotate in regular orbits.

Behind the Scenes

- When United Airlines was sponsoring the Tiki Room at Disneyland, the company raised a complaint over the Astro Orbitor's name (which was then "Astro Jets") because it was the name that American Airlines used for a certain class of aircraft in its fleet. In a demonstration of United's influence over Disneyland at the time, the name was changed to "Tomorrowland Jets" in 1964.
- The Rocket Jets version of the attraction opened in 1967 and was located on an elevated platform in the center of Tomorrowland. However, when the Astro Orbitor version was installed in 1998, it needed to be at ground level due to its size, so it was placed at the entrance to Tomorrowland.

Astro Orbitor

Things to Look For

- Each rocket lands next to a design that corresponds to a sign of the zodiac. There are twelve rockets so the entire astrological year is covered.
- A machine called the Observatron was installed in the location that the Rocket Jets formerly occupied, and parts from the Rocket Jets attraction were used in the machine's construction. It was intended to activate at timed intervals and appear to communicate with something in space, but it has always been plagued by technical difficulties.
- Many elements of the Astro Orbitor's appearance were inspired by the works of Jules Verne and Leonardo da Vinci.

Quick Facts

- Current version opened: May 22, 1998
- Original version opened: 1956
- Previously known as: "Astro Jets," "Tomorrowland Jets," and "Rocket Jets"
- Vehicle type: Orbiting rockets
- Number of vehicles: 12
- Ride length: Approximately 1.5 minutes

Autopia

About the Attraction

Autopia was originally designed to model the new interstate highway system that was being developed at the time, but now that interstate highways are commonplace, Autopia has become less of a futuristic experience. The attraction allows guests to race through a course with two separate tracks, and is the only Tomorrowland attraction that has existed, in one form or another, since Opening Day in 1955.

Behind the Scenes

- Originally, Autopia had no center guide rail and drivers were free to maneuver as they pleased, but cars would often spin out or run off the track.
- Until 2000, there were separate Tomorrowland and Fantasyland Autopia tracks, but when Chevron signed on as a sponsor the two Autopias were combined into the single Tomorrowland ride.
- The Autopia cars are gas powered, as is certainly obvious to all who smell the gasoline fumes around the track. However, it is rumored that a switch to electric power is imminent.

Autopia

Things to Look For

- The three different Autopia car models include Dusty, the all-terrain vehicle, Sparky, the sports car, and Suzy, the coupe, and are patterned after the car mascots used in Chevron's ad campaigns.
- It is actually a very difficult challenge not to bump into the guide rail in the center of the road. Even very experienced drivers have trouble avoiding it, so give it a shot for some extra fun.
- When you come to the Mouse Crossing sign, look across the street and you will see a mouse hole.
- Look for a roadside statue of a car from the retired Junior Autopia attraction and a statue of a vehicle from Mr. Toad's Wild Ride.

Quick Facts

- Opened: July 17, 1955 (opened with Disneyland Park)
- Origin of name: "Automobile" + "Utopia"
- Originally sponsored by: Richfield Oil
- Currently sponsored by: Chevron
- Maximum vehicle speed: 7 mph
- Track lengths: 2,555 ft. and 2,568 ft.

Buzz Lightyear Astro Blasters

About the Attraction

The Buzz Lightyear Astro Blasters attraction combines the mechanics of a dark ride with the gameplay of a video game. Guests use laser guns to hit targets and gain points as they progress through

the ride and compete for a ranking on the daily high scores table.

Behind the Scenes

- The Buzz Lightyear animatronic figure in the ride queue incorporates a similar effect as Madame Leota in the Haunted Mansion. That is, facial features are digitally projected onto an otherwise featureless head.
- The physical ride networks with a corresponding internet video game, and allows internet-based players to activate targets that give more points to players at the attraction in person.
- The ride gives a small amount of points to guests even if they continue to miss so that nobody is left with a score of zero.

Buzz Lightyear Astro Blasters

Things to Look For

- The maximum displayable score is 999,999 points, but guests who have scores greater than that can view their actual scores on their ride photos.
- The targets do not deactivate when the ride stops to allow a handicapped guest to board, so make sure to keep firing away during any pauses.
- Circle targets are 100 points, squares are 1,000 points, diamonds are 5,000 points, and triangles are 10,000 points.
- There are a few hidden or unmarked targets in the attraction. The hole in the center of Zerg's armor is an unmarked target. There are also four hidden targets in the dark tunnel: a triangle on the right as you move into the tunnel, a triangle on the left as you leave it, and two diamonds on the ceiling.

Quick Facts

- Opened: March, 2005
- Vehicle type: Guest-controllable XP-40 Star Cruiser
- Vehicle capacity: 2
- Ride length: Approximately 5 minutes
- Ride system: Omnimover (continuous loading allowing for higher capacity)

Disneyland Monorail System

About the Attraction

The first monorail in the United States to operate on a consistent, daily schedule, the Disneyland Monorail System transports guests between stations in Tomorrowland and Downtown Disney. While it now functions as a useful transport system, the monorail originally operated in a loop with no destination, serving only as futuristic entertainment.

Behind the Scenes

- Walt's original idea for the Disneyland Monorail was for it to be an example of how clean public transportation could be implemented in the future. He had hoped that major cities would adopt the monorail concept, and even invited several Los Angles transportation officials to ride the Disneyland Monorail, but wide-scale adoption of monorail technology never occurred to any significant degree.
- Estimates put the original cost of laying the Disneyland Monorail track at approximately one million dollars per mile.

Disneyland Monorail System

- The monorail storage and repair area is on the upper story of the Disneyland Railroad roundhouse located behind the "It's a Small World" building.

Things to Look For

- There is a chance that the pilot will allow a guest or two to ride along in the control area on some trips. Your best bet for securing such a ride is to ask a Cast Member at the station before you board.
- In its journey over Tomorrowland and around the Matterhorn, the Disneyland Monorail travels significantly farther than is required to reach its destination. This is in tune with the general sentiment that monorail technology is suited more for show purposes than practical use.

Quick Facts

- Opened: June 14, 1959
- Total track length: 2.5 Miles
- Maximum trains in operation at once: 3
- Round trip ride length: Approximately 15 minutes
- Powered by: A series of electric motors along the length of each train

Finding Nemo Submarine Voyage

About the Attraction

Replacing the original Submarine Voyage attraction, Finding Nemo Submarine Voyage takes guests on an underwater journey to explore a volcano. Along the way, they encounter characters and scenes from the 2003 Pixar film *Finding Nemo*.

Behind the Scenes

- A large part of the color in the underwater landscape comes from the use of recycled glass, which is much more durable than paint and allowed Imagineers to create many unique new colors.
- The submarines used in the previous version of the attraction were extensively adapted for the new version. This included the installation of electric motors to replace the previous diesel engines. The new electric motors use inductive power transfer, which allows them to be supplied with electricity wirelessly using electromagnetic coils, thereby eliminating the need for any direct contact with the power source.

Finding Nemo Submarine Voyage

Things to Look For

- There is an "observation station" that allows guests who are unable or unwilling to ride in the submarines to view the ride on a high-definition screen.
- Look for the greedy seagulls from the movie on a buoy in the lagoon.
- When you see the diver who is taking pictures of the fish, look closely at his mask. Just like in the movie, his address is written there: 42 Wallaby Way, Sydney.
- The captain's comment about sea serpents and mermaids is a reference to the creatures featured in the original Submarine Voyage. As he makes this remark, look for the sea serpent-shaped coral.

Quick Facts

- Opened: June, 2007
- Vehicle type: Boat with underwater cabin, giving the experience of a submarine
- Vehicle capacity: 40
- Number of vehicles: 8
- Ride length: Approximately 13 minutes
- Lagoon capacity: 6.3 million gallons

Honey, I Shrunk the Audience

About the Attraction

Honey, I Shrunk the Audience is an immersive 3D show based on the series of "Honey..." films starring Rick Moranis as a semi-eccentric inventor. The plot centers around the Inventor of the Year Award Ceremonies at the Imagination Institute, which takes a turn for the worse as Professor Szalinski's shrinking machine is turned on the audience.

Behind the Scenes

- Like many other 3D attractions, Honey, I Shrunk the Audience makes use of polarized glasses which control the images that each eye sees in order to create artificial depth perception.
- When the theater is shaken, the entire audience seating area is lifted several inches by powerful mechanisms to create the effect.
- The scurrying mice effect uses compressed air channeled through a number of tubes located under the seats.

Honey, I Shrunk the Audience

- Honey, I Shrunk the Audience was directed by Randal Kleiser, who also directed *Honey, I Blew Up the Kid* in 1992.

Things to Look For

- Look for a small hole on the back of the seat in front of you. This is where the water for the dog sneeze effect comes out.
- The show features several members of the cast of the original "Honey..." movies. In addition to Rick Moranis as Wayne Szalinski, Robert Oliveri plays Nick Szalinski and Marcia Strassman plays Diane Szalinski.

Quick Facts

- Opened: May 22, 1998
- Replaced: Captain EO
- Show length: Approximately 20 minutes
- Host: Dr. Nigel Channing (played by Eric Idle from Monty Python)
- Starring: Rick Moranis as Wayne Szalinski
- Sponsor: Kodak

Innoventions

About the Attraction

Occupying the same building as the previous attractions Carousel of Progress and America Sings, Innoventions takes a look at present and future technological development in a series of exhibits, many sponsored by various high-tech oriented companies.

Behind the Scenes

- The part of the Innoventions building that rotates is a separate ring on the outside bottom floor.
- In 1974, when the building was still occupied by America Sings, a Cast Member was killed when she became trapped between the walls of the non-moving and moving portions of the building. These walls have since been replaced and will now give way if something is lodged between them.

Things to Look For

- See what vintage Tomorrowland attractions you can spot on the outside murals as you wait to step inside Innoventions.

Innoventions

- Even when no guests are around and his show is over, Tom Morrow continues to shift about in a life-like manner. You can see this if you stick around for a bit after he finishes his presentation.
- Tom Morrow is wearing his own Cast Member name tag.
- The song "There's a Great Big Beautiful Tomorrow" that host Tom Morrow sings is a tribute to the original Carousel of Progress attraction, which featured the song prominently in its show.
- Upstairs there was previously an area where you could talk to Stitch from the 2002 film *Lilo & Stitch*. It was an interactive experience similar to Turtle Talk with Crush in Disney's California Adventure. Both attractions use a new technique of synchronizing an animated character's movements to the voice of a Cast Member backstage.

Quick Facts

- Opened: November, 1998
- Lower section rotation speed: 6 inches per second (one rotation approximately every 17 minutes)
- Host: Tom Morrow, voiced by Nathan Lane (the voice of Timon in *The Lion King*)
- Prominent sponsors: Pioneer, ESPN, Honda

Space Mountain

About the Attraction

Space Mountain is an indoor roller coaster with the theme of a flight through space. Much of the ride takes place in a room that is dark except for the presence of stars, which adds a great deal to the excitement of the roller coaster itself.

Behind the Scenes

- When Space Mountain originally opened, it was the first roller coaster to have safety controls and restrictions monitored and enforced completely by computer equipment.
- The Space Mountain building is actually sunken about 15 ft. into the ground, which keeps it from appearing excessively tall above ground.
- The soundtrack on Space Mountain is synchronized exactly with each rocket's location along the roller coaster track. Even if a rocket slows down or is delayed, the soundtrack will adjust accordingly.
- The overhead clearance in Space Mountain can be quite low, and although your head is safe, holding your hands in the air may not always be wise.

Space Mountain

Things to Look For

- The spaceport from which riders take off is designated as "Space Station 77" in recognition of the year that Space Mountain first opened.
- The shape of the space vessel suspended above the ride vehicle loading area is a nod to Stanley Kubrick's *2001: A Space Odyssey* (1968), which featured a similarly elongated and partitioned spaceship on which the main characters travelled.
- Look up as you pull away from the station and you will be able to see a ride operator control room. If you can catch their eye and wave, they will often wave back.
- To the left of the track as you pull away from the station, you can see the side track that is used to put rockets onto the main track and take them off.

Quick Facts

- Opened: May 27, 1977
- Vehicle type: Space rocket
- Vehicle capacity: 12 (6 Rows of 2)
- Ride length: Approximately 3 minutes
- Top speed: Approximately 30 mph
- Highest point on mountain: 117 ft.
- Past sponsors: RCA, FedEx

Star Tours

About the Attraction

Based on the series of *Star Wars* films, Star Tours uses a motion simulator to take guests on a trip to Endor. The journey goes awry thanks to an inexperienced pilot and passengers find themselves in a series of tight situations throughout the Star Wars universe.

Behind the Scenes

- Both in the queue and in the ride itself, C3PO is voiced by Anthony Daniels, the actor who filled the role of C3PO in all six Star Wars episodes.
- The simulator platforms that were adapted for use in Star Tours were originally designed for military and commercial flight training, but Star Tours designers saw their potential for mass entertainment.
- George Lucas has confirmed that Star Tours II, an overhaul of Star Tours, is in the works and will likely incorporate elements from *Star Wars* episodes I, II, and III. It is also planned to feature a replacement of the current film with a digital 3D version and possibly allow for as much as 6° of simulator movement (rather than the current 3°).

Star Tours

Things to Look For

- In the queue, listen for a voice paging "Egroeg Sacul" ("George Lucas" spelled backwards) and Tom Morrow, the host of Innoventions.
- There is also a voice page concerning a speeder with license number THX 1138. This is the name of George Lucas' first major film.
- Look for a red "Remove Before Flight" tag on Rex the pilot.
- Listen for Rex's line "I have a very bad feeling about this," a famous line from the *Star Wars* films.
- A few employees from the Industrial Light & Magic team that worked on the ride are visible in the film. Look for them as dock workers and in the window that Rex comes close to crashing through at the end of the trip.

Quick Facts

- Opened: January 9, 1987
- Vehicle type: Starspeeder 3000
- Number of vehicles: 4
- Vehicle capacity: 40
- Ride length: Approximately 4.5 minutes
- Current sponsor: Panasonic
- Previous sponsors: M&M's, Energizer

Adventureland

Indiana Jones Adventure

Ancient Statue

Just before you reach the drinking fountain in the attraction's queue, look for a tri-circle Hidden Mickey carved into the stone at the base of a small, black statue on a pedestal.

Difficulty to find: 3/10 | Rating: 4/10

Magazine Mickey

Tucked away inside Indiana Jones' office beyond the projector room is an old copy of *Life* magazine from the 1930's. See if you can spot a drawing of Mickey on the magazine's cover.

Difficulty to find: 4/10 | Rating: 6/10

Indiana Jones Adventure

Mara's Philtrum

Once on the ride, pay close attention to the figure of Mara's head above you as the vehicle passes through one of the three doors. His nostrils and philtrum (the indentation above his upper lip) form a Hidden Mickey.

Difficulty to find: 5/10 | Rating: 7/10

Bones the Skeleton

As you enter the skeleton room, look to the left of the vehicle and you may be able to catch a quick glimpse of Bones the Skeleton. He is located just inside the entrance to the room and wears a Mickey hat on his head. Like Harold at the Matterhorn, Bones is well known among Cast Members, so questions such as "How is Harold doing today?" are likely to illicit fun responses.

Difficulty to find: 9/10 | Rating: 8/10

Jungle Cruise

Suwannee Lady

The Suwannee Lady boat has a frying pan hanging from its side. There is a Hidden Mickey on the pan that gives the impression that it has been used frequently to make Mickey pancakes.

Note: This Hidden Mickey may not always be visible as the Suwannee Lady does not operate every day.

Difficulty to find: 4/10 | Rating: 8/10

Tarzan's Treehouse

Treehouse Curtains

In the area where Jane is sketching a drawing of Tarzan, the coils at the ends of the ropes holding up the curtains form a number of Hidden Mickeys along the walls of the room.

Difficulty to find: 2/10 | Rating: 7/10

Jungle Drums

As you come down from the treehouse, see if you can get a good view of the table on the ground behind the treehouse that holds a variety of musical instruments. From above, it is easy to spot a Mickey formed from the drums.

Difficulty to find: 3/10 | Rating: 5/10

Walt Disney's Enchanted Tiki Room

Bird Perches

There are several Hidden Mickeys that can be found in the designs of the bird cages and perches. See how many you can identify. The most obvious ones are on the birdmobile branches.

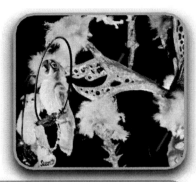

Difficulty to find: 7/10 | Rating: 4/10

Hina Kuluua

Look for a Hidden Mickey on the Hina Kuluua sign in the Tiki Garden before the show begins. While this is a fairly convincing Mickey, it is questionable because of the large separation between head and ears.

Difficulty to find: 2/10 | Rating: 3/10

Critter Country

The Many Adventures of Winnie the Pooh

Honey Bubbles

Between the "Heffalumps and Woozles" scene and the "Birthday" scene, look closely at the string of honey bubbles around the Heffalumps on the right side. A very distinct Hidden Mickey hides within the sugary trail.

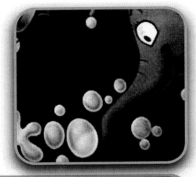

Difficulty to find: 5/10 | Rating: 8/10

Pooh Corner Lollipop Stand

Pooh Corner is one of several shops throughout Disneyland that use multi-level stands for lollipops or other merchandise. Often, these stands are covered with dozens of Hidden Mickeys cut into their center poles.

Difficulty to find: 2/10 | Rating: 6/10

Splash Mountain

Grinding Gears

As you enter the indoor portion of the queue (the "barn"), look to your left and see if you can spot the Hidden Mickey made out of rusty gears. You may have to bend down to see it straight on and get the full effect.

Difficulty to find: 3/10 | Rating: 7/10

Flower Patches

Mickeys lurk within the flower patches through-out the ride, so pay atten-tion to them and see how many flowery Mickeys you can find. One good place to look is the flower patch to the right as you approach the steamboat.

Difficulty to find: 6/10 | Rating: 4/10

Alice in Wonderland

Paint Drop Mickey

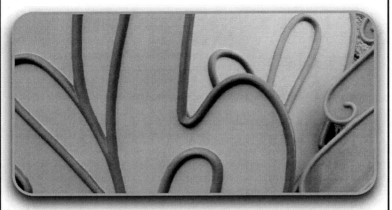

As you pass through the "painting the roses red" scene, look at the bushes on the left. On top of a small hedge located near a card climbing a ladder is a Hidden Mickey formed from the paint drops of the cards' messy handiwork.

Difficulty to find: 6/10 | Rating: 8/10

Castle Heraldry Shoppe

Shoppe Mailbox

Take a close look at the mailbox outside of the Castle Heraldry Shoppe. The vines that are drawn around its edges converge to form a Hidden Mickey at the bottom of the mailbox, just below the letter 'A' in "Mail."

Difficulty to find: 3/10 | Rating: 9/10

Gavin Family Crest

Within the shop itself, a variety of family crests are on display. The one representing the Gavin family contains what is often mistaken for a Hidden Mickey. In reality, however, this Mickey-like shape is a feature on the actual Gavin family crest, which was originally created hundreds of years before Mickey even existed.

As such, the Gavin crest in the Castle Heraldry Shoppe serves as an excellent example of the tendency to immediately label any tri-circle pattern in Disneyland as a Hidden Mickey.

King Arthur Carrousel

Jingles

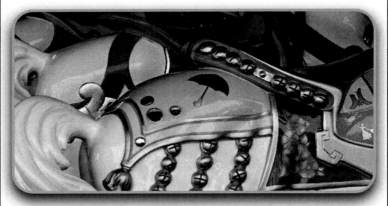

Jingles is often considered to be the Carrousel's lead horse, as it is the only one covered in decorative bells. In addition to the bells, Jingles is wearing a variety of jewels, a few of which combine to form multiple Mickey shapes. These are some of the most well-known Hidden Mickeys in the park.

Difficulty to find: 3/10 | Rating: 8/10

Mr. Toad's Wild Ride

The Statue's Eye

After you enter the in-door portion of the queue (inside Toad Hall), look for the statue of Mr. Toad by the window. A distinct Hidden Mickey is painted in red on the bottom of each of Mr. Toad's eyes.

Difficulty to find: 4/10 | Rating: 7/10

Leaded Glass Door

Near the start of the ride, look for a Hidden Mickey on the left leaded glass pane in the set of doors near where you burst through the fireplace. This Mickey is very difficult to spot, as it is small and moves out of the way quickly.

Difficulty to find: 9/10 | Rating: 6/10

Peter Pan's Flight

Flying Over London

While soaring above the London cityscape, there are two Hidden Mickeys to keep an eye out for. One is imprinted in the markings on the moon above and the other is located on the model of Big Ben below. Among the lights of the giant clock tower, it is possible to see a silhouette of Mickey standing within one of the many windows.

Difficulty to find: 7/10 | Rating: 6/10

Pinocchio's Daring Journey

Popcorn Kernels

As you pass through the
Pleasure Island area,
keep an eye out for two
Hidden Mickeys made
out of popcorn kernels.
There is a small Mickey
in the popcorn machine
and a larger one on the
ground below it.

Difficulty to find: 4/10 | Rating: 8/10

Geppetto's Workshop

In the Geppetto's workshop scene there is a wooden
case holding a large ship model. You may have to
look back over your shoulder to spot it, as it is located right next to a turn in the ride track. Look
closely at the woodwork on the top of this case and
you may be able to spot a Hidden Mickey carved
into it.

Difficulty to find: 4/10 | Rating: 5/10

Snow White's Scary Adventures

Loading Area Mural

There is a questionable Hidden Mickey among the bushes in the painted mural by the loading area. You be the judge of whether this is a true Hidden Mickey or an unintentional one.

Difficulty to find: 4/10 | Rating: 3/10

Turtle Shell

Near the starting point of the ride, watch for the stairs to the left of the vehicle and take a close look at the turtle climbing up them. If you see him from the right angle, you can "spot" this Hidden Mickey.

Difficulty to find: 5/10 | Rating: 8/10

Storybook Land Canal Boats

Cave of Wonders

As you enter the cave of wonders, keep your eye on the piles of treasure to the right side of the boat. There is a very tiny Mickey made out of little jewels, but it is resting close to a larger golden pot that you should be able to locate much more easily. This Mickey is very difficult to see, but once you have found the golden pot, it should be much easier.

Difficulty to find: 8/10 | Rating: 8/10

Village Haus Restaurant

Stained Glass Pattern

To the left of the entrance to the Village Haus are a series of stained glass panels. Look for a group of yellow Mickey shapes within the pattern on one of these panels. Note that these could easily just be trefoils and not Mickeys.

Difficulty to find: 2/10 | Rating: 3/10

High Chairs

Some of the wooden high chairs in the Village Haus have Mickeys carved into them rather than the more common heart design. These Mickey cutouts can be found in a few other park restaurants as well.

Difficulty to find: 3/10 | Rating: 6/10

Frontierland

Big Thunder Mountain Railroad

Rusty Gears

As you emerge from the cave with the rainbow pools, look to the left of the track to see a very evident Hidden Mickey made out of old, rusty gears lying to the side of the mine train track.

Difficulty to find: 3/10 | Rating: 8/10

Slithering Mickeys

On the following lift hill, keep an eye out along the canyon walls for snakes curled up into Mickey-like shapes. These slithering Mickeys are best viewed from above, so look quickly as you make your way over the hill.

Difficulty to find: 6/10 | Rating: 5/10

Golden Horseshoe

Stage Grating

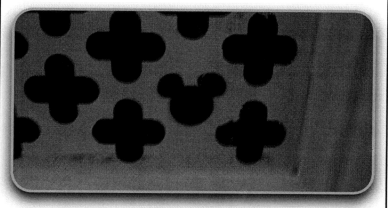

A personal favorite Hidden Mickey, this one is both very hard to stumble upon if you are not specifically looking for it and very impressive once found. The best time to see it is in between shows in the Golden Horseshoe.

If you can find a time when the theater is mostly empty, walk all the way up to the first row and look closely at the panels of grating beneath the stage. In the corner of one of the panels, the pattern of the grate is modified to form a very satisfying Hidden Mickey.

Difficulty to find: 4/10 | Rating: 10/10

Mark Twain Riverboat

"River Excursions"

Near the ship dock on the Rivers of America is a small structure with a mural advertising "River Excursions" painted on its side. Look closely and see if you can find Mickey riding the steamboat in the mural.

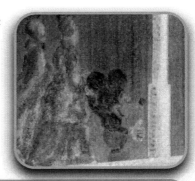

Difficulty to find: 5/10 | Rating: 7/10

Riverboat Ironwork

In the ironwork connecting the smokestacks of the Mark Twain is a somewhat distorted Mickey. This is a questionable Hidden Mickey due to its odd shape, but it can be fairly convincing from some angles.

Difficulty to find: 3/10 | Rating: 3/10

Park Entrance

Turnstile Speaker

Hidden on the back side of the turnstiles at the park's entrance is a Mickey-shaped speaker that plays the chimes when a guest enters the park. This is an impressive Hidden Mickey due to its perfect shape.

Difficulty to find: 2/10 | Rating: 8/10

"Strollers & Wheelchairs"

Just inside and directly to the right of the park entrance is the building for stroller and wheelchair rentals. On the sides of the sign for this building are two Hidden Mickeys formed from curls cut out of the wood.

Difficulty to find: 3/10 | Rating: 7/10

"Partners" Statue

Mickey Ring

Walt Disney, as depicted in the "Partners" statue at the end of Main Street, has a Mickey ring on one of his fingers. It is not easy to spot, as it is fairly small and is sculpted in the same color and material as the rest of the statue, but if you look closely, you should be able to see its outline.

Difficulty to find: 5/10 | Rating: 5/10

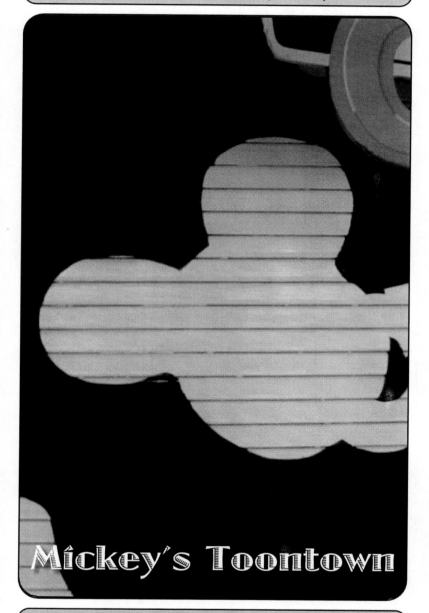

Mickey's Toontown

Character Houses

Publisher Marks

Throughout Mickey and Minnie's houses, look for books with Mickey-shaped publisher marks on their spines.
Bonus: Search Minnie's House for a Hidden Mickey mark on a bottle of "cheese relish."

Difficulty to find: 3/10 | Rating: 6/10

Mickey's Piano

Take a close look at the piano in Mickey's House and you will see that it is full of Hidden Mickeys. Its paper tape is punched with Mickey-shaped holes and its metronome is decorated with a Mickey symbol.

Difficulty to find: 3/10 | Rating: 7/10

Clarabelle's Frozen Yogurt

Cowhide Spots

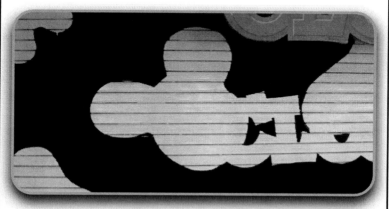

When the frozen yogurt stand is closed, a patterned covering of cowhide-like black and white splotches is pulled over the front of the stand. Among the features on this covering is a spot in the form of a tri-circle Hidden Mickey.

Difficulty to find: 4/10 | Rating: 8/10

Gadget's Go Coaster

Queue Walls

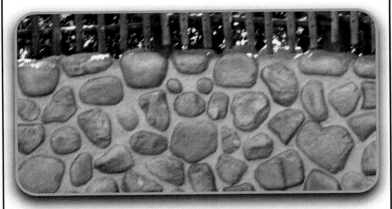

For a large portion of the Gadget's Go Coaster queue, the line is bordered by walls of assorted stones. Throughout these areas of the queue, look for Hidden Mickeys inlaid into the walls with tri-circle formations of stones such as the one pictured above.

Difficulty to find: 3/10 | Rating: 8/10

Roger Rabbit's Car Toon Spin

Manhole Covers

There are manhole covers located throughout the attraction queue that incorporate subtle Hidden Mickeys into the patterns of indentations on their metal surfaces.

Difficulty to find: 4/10 | Rating: 6/10

Hubcap and Gauges

After you have been loaded into the taxicab ride vehicles, keep an eye out on the right side of the track as you proceed out of the loading area. Look for a Hidden Mickey made out of hubcaps and gauges.

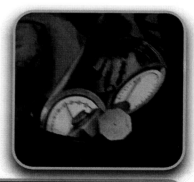

Difficulty to find: 6/10 | Rating: 6/10

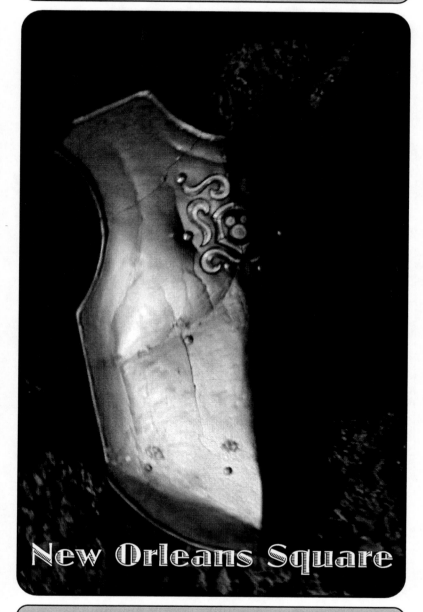

New Orleans Square

Cristal d'Orleans

Tile Designs

Near the shop's entrance that faces the back side of New Orleans Square (away from the Rivers of America), look along the tile threshold for a Mickey that stands out in brilliant red and blue.

This Hidden Mickey is questionable because one of its ears is outlined in front of its head while its other ear appears behind its head. However, the shape is so convincing that this one may be a valid Mickey.

Difficulty to find: 3/10 | Rating: 4/10

Haunted Mansion

Ghostly Table Settings

While not hard to spot, this Hidden Mickey is very fun to find, and is something that you will not be able to avoid noticing once you know it's there. When the ride passes above the grand ballroom, take a close look at the table settings below. Some of the places at the table are set in classic tri-circle Mickey fashion, with a large plate and two smaller plates making up the formation.

Difficulty to find: 4/10 | Rating: 8/10

Pirates of the Caribbean

Captain's Bed

In the captain's bedroom scene, look among the piles of gold and treasure for the captain's bed. Carved out of its wood is a tri-circle Mickey shape that protrudes from the top of the bed's back. There is also a possible Hidden Mickey in the captain's chair nearby.

Difficulty to find: 7/10 | Rating: 5/10

Cannonball Blasts

As you pass the pirates firing on the Spanish town, look along the fort wall for a Hidden Mickey made from the impact of cannonballs on the bricks of the wall. This Mickey is easiest to see as you are turning into the fort.

Difficulty to find: 6/10 | Rating: 7/10

Pirates of the Caribbean

Armor Plating

Near the end of the ride, you will encounter a pirate riding on top of a cannon, engaged in a pistol battle. Look behind this pirate at the gold armor plate for a very small and extremely difficult to spot Hidden Mickey.

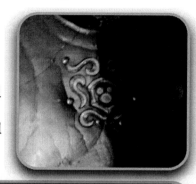

Difficulty to find: 9/10 | Rating: 8/10

Treasure Map Mickey

When you pass the small island with the parrot at the very end of the ride, take a close look at the upper-right corner of the treasure map for an elusive Hidden Mickey formed from jewels in a pile of treasure.

Difficulty to find: 9/10 | Rating: 5/10

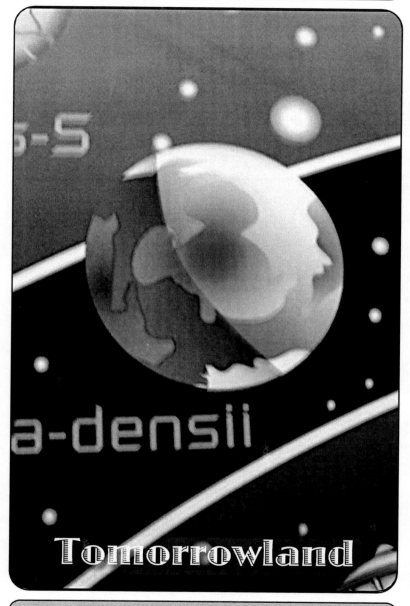

Autopia

Registration Stickers

Each Autopia car has a registration sticker attached to its license plate. If you look closely at these stickers, you can see a tri-circle Mickey design printed on them.

Bonus: Keep an eye out for the "Mouse Crossing" sign with a silhouette of Mickey as you make your way through the track.

Difficulty to find: 4/10 | Rating: 6/10

Buzz Lightyear Astro Blasters

Star Charts

After you enter the indoor portion of the queue, look along the walls at the star charts. Check for a uniquely-shaped continent on the planet labeled "Ska-densii," and a similar pattern on "Green Planet."

Difficulty to find: 4/10 | Rating: 7/10

Falling Tile

As your vehicle enters the second turn, look ahead along the wall for a red robot with flames coming out of his feet. Below this robot is a falling tile with a tri-circle Mickey design painted on it.

Difficulty to find: 7/10 | Rating: 7/10

Innoventions

Miscellaneous Mickeys

- In the entertainment section on the outside of the Innoventions building, look for both a Hidden Mickey displayed on a monitor and a Mickey made out of planets in the painted sky.
- Robotic host Tom Morrow has little Hidden Mickeys all over his shoelaces.
- Inside the new house of the future portion of Innoventions, look for a set of Hidden Mickeys in the design of some latticework underneath a pair of railings.

Difficulty to find: 5/10 | Rating: 5/10

Space Mountain

Vehicle Speakers

This is a fun, easy to spot Hidden Mickey in a place that you may have glanced at on numerous occasions, but never noticed the Mickey in plain sight. Each pair of seats on the Space Mountain ride vehicles has a trio of speakers behind it. Look at the perfect tri-circle Mickey formed by the speakers' shapes.

Difficulty to find: 3/10 | Rating: 7/10

Star Tours

Mickey Doll

In the flight safety instruction video that is shown before boarding the Star Tours ship, watch the first Ewok to appear on the screen among the crowd of humans and aliens that enter the vessel. He is carrying a Mickey doll in his hands, which he must later stow in the compartment under his seat.

Bonus: It is debatable, but many people consider the flight attendant's hair in the pre-boarding video to be a Hidden Mickey as well, with her two buns forming the ears as if she were wearing a Mickey hat on the side of her head.

Difficulty to find: 6/10 | Rating: 6/10

Queue Games

Indiana Jones Adventure

See if you can rearrange the following items into the order in which they appear in the Indiana Jones Adventure queue. Write the letters corresponding to each item in the ordered blanks below.

D. A clock indicating "Indy Time."

E. Stacked crates on their way to Nang Toa Airport and Oxford University.

N. Map of Asia.

R. Coins pouring out of a goblet.

O. Sign that says "TAKE HEED!"

I. Advisory concerning the diamond-shaped stones.

S. Silver lantern on a barrel to the left of a hanging green lantern.

J. Rope that must not be pulled.

1. [__] 2. [__] 3. [__] 4. [__]

5. [__] 6. [__] 7. [__] 8. [__]

Walt Disney's Enchanted Tiki Room

Guess the Hawaiian Tiki God: The following clues narrow down the possibilities to only one of the Tiki Gods in the Tiki Room's waiting garden. See if you can eliminate the wrong choices and guess which Tiki God it is.

1. I am not sticking my tongue out.
2. Unlike one of my fellow Tiki Gods, I don't "rock and roll."
3. I do not have one or more winged creatures perched upon my head.
4. I am not known for putting native spectators into a trance.
5. I'm not carrying anything edible on my head.
6. I am not the one who is responsible for making the orchids bloom.

Choices

Hina Kuluua   Koro   Maui   Ngendei

Pele   Rongo   Tangaroa   Tangaroa-Ru

Answer: _____

Splash Mountain

The following is the text from a sign seen multiple times in the Splash Mountain queue. However, each letter has been switched with another letter in the alphabet. Compare the original sign with the version quoted below to figure out the letter pairings. Next, use this knowledge to decode the question at the bottom of the page, which can then be answered with information from the Splash Mountain ride.

fyyjsynts!
knkyd ktty uqzslj fmjfi
xuqfxm rtzsyfns nx f yzwgzqjsy kqzrj fiajsyzwj bnym mnlm
xujjix, mjnlmyx, xziijs iwtux fsi xytux!
nk dtz hmttxj yt wnij, dtz rzxy wjrfns xjfyji izwnsl ymj
jsynwj wnij.
dtz rfd jcny mjwj

Question: Bmfy gjsi hfs gj wjfhmji gd ywfajqnsl ns ymj tuutxnyj inwjhynts tk Itt Ifm Qfsinsl?

Translated question: _____

_____

_____?

Answer: _____

Matterhorn Bobsleds

Below is a diagram of the coats of arms that are mounted on the pillars throughout the queue. The coats of arms in the diagram face outward, away from the mountain. Each clue below describes one of the coats of arms. Use the diagram to find the letter associated with each coat of arms and write that letter in the corresponding blank at the bottom of the page to reveal a question. If you need help answering this question, ask any Matterhorn Cast Member.

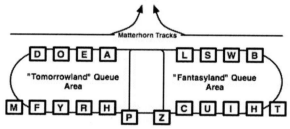

1. Single key facing to the left.
2. Bundle of poles and an axe.
3. Red nose ring.
4. Stars split down the middle.
5. Four hooves, a red tongue, and a stylish hat.
6. Climbing up a red hill with tongue curled out.
7. Half black, half white.
8. Text that begins with its letter on the diagram.
9. A saintly figure.

__ __ __ __ __ __ __ __ __ __ __ ?
1 2 3 4 5 2 6 7 3 8 9

Answer: _____

Peter Pan's Flight

There is a message hidden within the design of the Peter Pan's Flight building, but to read it you need to use a special decoding system. Each of the following questions will have a number as an answer. You can translate these numbers into letters using the decoder below. Write the letter answers from each question in the blanks at the bottom of the page to reveal the hidden message.

4	2	6	2	1		4	5	3
P	**E**	**T**	**E**	**R**		**P**	**A**	**N**

(a) The number of green-framed windows directly above the entrance to the attraction.

(b) The number of chimneys on the rooftop to the right of the Peter Pan clock tower.

(c) The number of **red** windowsill flower boxes in the same part of the building.

(d) The number of feathers in Peter Pan's hat on the attraction's logo.

(e) The number of circles on the face of the clock tower clock (don't count the outermost circle that surrounds the entire clock face).

(f) The number of masts on the ship depicted in the clock tower's weathervane.

___ ___ ___ ___ ___ ___ ___ ___ ___
(a) (b)   (c) (d)   (e) (f)

Big Thunder Mountain Railroad

The following quotes are very similar to ones found in the Big Thunder Mountain Railroad queue. Find the word or phrase in each quote below that differs from what is written in the attraction queue and write it in the corresponding blank. The result will be a clue with an answer that can be found in the Thunder Mountain ride.

1. "Chemical analyses of every color made with accuracy and dispatch."
2. "Hang on to your hats and glasses, 'cause this here's the wildest ride of the wilderness!"
3. "The Big Thunder Mine / 1880"
4. "Big Thunder 50 ft.
   Spiral Butte 1/4 mi.
   Goat's Canyon 1/2 mi."
5. "Poker • Billiards / Food & Dancing"

_____ (1) _____ (2) _____ (3)

_____ (4) _____ (5)

Answer: _____

Disneyland Railroad

From which of the four stations on the Disneyland Railroad circuit can you spot each of the following items?

1. A rectangular, green luggage bag with brown and blue patches on it.
2. Small blue, and large white tent-style coverings on buildings to the left and right of the station.
3. An unlucky elevator with yellow doors and a semi-circular window over it.
4. Red buckets labeled "for fire only."
5. A monorail station.
6. A sign with the word "HUNGRY" in large letters.
7. A red, white, and green awning over a dining area.
8. A wooden cart with red wheels carrying a load of luggage trunks.
9. Various musical instruments resting on a second-floor balcony.
10. A wooden water tower with a giant "M" painted onto it.

Main Street, U.S.A.: _____

New Orleans Square: _____

Mickey's Toontown: _____

Tomorrowland: _____

Gadget's Go Coaster

Gadget is getting ready to build a new contraption out of some of the spare parts laying around her Go Coaster. However, she wants to make sure that the colors of these parts will go well together when the contraption is assembled. To help with this, Gadget created a formula that will add up to an important year for Chip 'n Dale if the colors are correct.

1. Start with the number **1900**.
2. If the letters on Gadget's beach towel are red, add **50**. If the letters are blue, add **100**.
3. If the pencil holding up Gadget's roof is pink with a yellow eraser, add **7**. If it is yellow with a pink eraser, add **4**.
4. If the acorn on Gadget's can of acorn soup is red, subtract **20**. If it is gold, subtract **10**.
5. If the glove turning the Go Coaster's mechanical hand crank is white, add **50**. If the glove is brown, add **40**.
6. If Gadget's spitting frogs are green with off-white bellies, add **5**. If they are off-white with green bellies, subtract **5**.
7. If the pipes coming down from the workshop's gutters have red stripes, subtract **10**. If the pipes have yellow stripes, subtract **5**.

Make all the calculations for a final total: _____

Roger Rabbit's Car Toon Spin

Use the answers to the following questions to fill in the spaces below. The boxed letters will reveal a notable quote from the ride.

1. The ID on the Toontown license plate with the numbers 19 and 32 (ignore spaces).
2. Character scheduled to perform the warm-up act at 9, 10:30, and midnight.
3. The second of two performers listed for a ballet performance as the fourth act.
4. Type of actors that need not apply for a part in "Melody Time."
5. What can be checked out by seeing the stage manager?
6. In order to avoid "The Dip," toons should do what in pairs?
7. The winner on the front page of "Racing Toon Form."
8. The third ingredient in "The Dip."

_ [_] [_] [_] (4)   [_] [_] _ _ _ (2)

[_] _ [_] _ _ _ (6)   [_] _ [_] _ _ (5)

_ _ [_] _ _ _ [_] _ _ _ (8)

_ _ [_] _ _ [_] _ _ [_] [_] (3)

[_] [_] _ _ _ _ (7)   [_] _ [_] _ _ _ (1)

Answer: _____

Haunted Mansion

Each of the following groups of words has one letter in common. Write these letters in their corresponding spaces below and then rearrange them to form a phrase relating to the Haunted Mansion.

1. The first five words on the sign inside the white hearse.
2. The type of animal that Rosie is and the type of animal that Buddy is.
3. The type of animal that Jeb is and the type of animal that Lilac is.
4. Levi's last name, Mr. Later's first name, and U.R.'s last name.
5. The color of the Haunted Mansion's front columns and the emotional state of the "haunts" inside the mansion.

[__] (1) [__] (4) [__] (4) [__] (3) [__] (2) [__] (5)

[__] (1) [__] (5) [__] (3)

" [__] [__] [__] [__] [__]   [__] [__] [__] [__] "

Pirates of the Caribbean

Use the answers to the following questions to fill in the spaces below. The boxed letters will reveal a notable quote from the ride.

1. What shape is below the text on the Pirates of the Caribbean sign at the queue entrance?
2. What anniversary is the fountain plaque dedicated to?
3. What is the last name of the second member of Walt Disney's Buccaneer Crew?
4. What color is Ned Low's necklace?
5. What drink is Sir Francis Verney holding?
6. What is drawn on the piece of parchment resting on the island with the parrot?
7. Whose "landing" do the boats launch from?

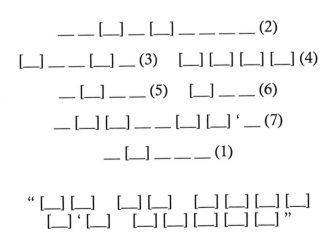

Space Mountain

Each of the clues below can be answered with a number. After you have found all of the answers, plug the resulting numbers into the formula at the bottom of the page to get a series of digits that is very important to Space Mountain.

A. The number of the airlock in Gantry 42.
B. The number of the airlock for exiting the space port near Gantry 42.
C. Fill in the blank: SMS – 0____.
D. The number of seats in each row on the Space Mountain ride vehicles.
E. Fill in the blank: DL 0__.
F. The number of double-door gates that open onto the track in the vehicle loading area.

I. $A + B - F$
II. $(E \times B) - F$
III. $A + E - D$
IV. $C - ((A + B) \times (D \times E))$

[__] [__] [__] [__]

(I)   (II) (III) (IV)

Star Tours

The following quotes are very similar to ones found in the Star Tours queue. Find the word or phrase in each quote below that differs from what is written *or spoken* in the attraction queue and write it in the corresponding blank. The result will be a question with an answer that can be found in the Star Tours ride.

1. "Star Tours announces the boarding of what is the Endor Express, non-stop StarSpeeder service to the moon of Endor."
2. "May I have your attention please? At this time, I'd like to take a moment to review your boarding process..."
3. "Most Flights to Endor! / 400 Convenient Star Tours Departures / New Moonlight Cruise"
4. "The exciting flight to Tatooine / Visit the galactic zoo / Drinks at the Mos Eisley Cantina"
5. "Arrivals/Departures

Number	Origin	Status
4	Hoth	Decontamination"

_____ (1) _____ (2) _____ (3)

_____ (4) _____ (5) ?

Answer: _____

Queue Game Solutions

Solutions

Adventureland

<u>Indiana Jones Adventure</u>

1.D 2.R 3.I 4.J 5.O 6.N 7.E 8.S

<u>Walt Disney's Enchanted Tiki Room</u>

1. Not Tangaroa
2. Not Ngendei
3. Not Tangaroa-Ru or Pele
4. Not Koro
5. Not Rongo
6. Not Hina Kuluua

Answer: Maui

Critter Country

<u>Splash Mountain</u>

Original Sign Text:
attention!
fifty foot plunge ahead
splash mountain is a turbulent flume adventure with high speeds, heights, sudden drops and stops!
if you choose to ride, you must remain seated during the entire ride.
you may exit here

Answer: Catfish Bend

Solutions

Fantasyland

<u>Matterhorn Bobsleds</u>

1.W 2.H 3.O 4.I 5.S 6.A 7.R 8.L 9.D

<u>Peter Pan's Flight</u>

a) 2 b) 2 c) 1 d) 5 e) 3   Answer: Neverland

Frontierland

<u>Big Thunder Mountain Railroad</u>

1. Color 2. of 3. the 4. goat's 5. food
Answer: Red

Main Street, U.S.A.

<u>Disneyland Railroad</u>

Main Street, U.S.A.: 4,8   New Orleans Square: 3,7,9
Mickey's Toontown: 1,2,10   Tomorrowland: 5,6

Mickey's Toontown

<u>Gadget's Go Coaster</u>

$1900 + 50 + 4 - 10 + 50 + 5 - 10 = 1989$
The year *Chip 'n Dale Rescue Rangers* debuted.

Solutions

Roger Rabbit's Car Toon Spin

1. LMERM8 2. Goofy 3. Clarabelle 4. Live
5. Props 6. Travel 7. Horace 8. Turpentine

New Orleans Square

Haunted Mansion

1.T 2.G 3.S 4.O 5.H
Answer: "Ghost Host"

Pirates of the Caribbean

1. Cross 2. Thirtieth 3. Baker 4. Gold 5. Wine
6. Map 7. Laffite's

Tomorrowland

Space Mountain

A.4 B.3 C.77 D.2 E.5 F.6
Answer: 1977, the year Space Mountain was built.

Star Tours

1. What is 2. your 3. Star Tours 4. flight
5. number

Made in the USA